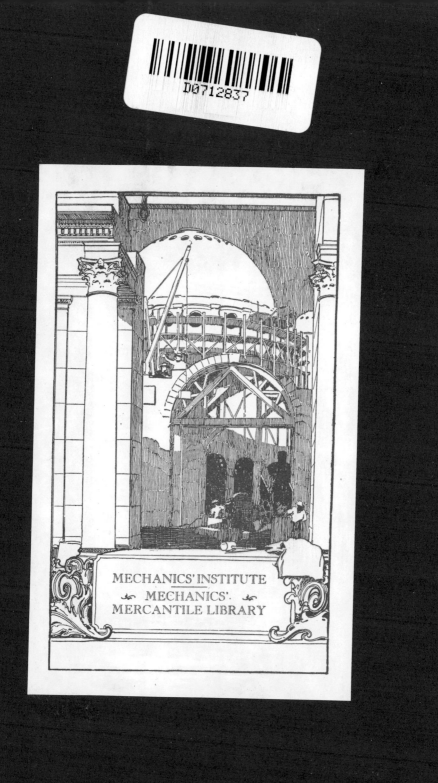

Bastard
in the
Ragged Suit

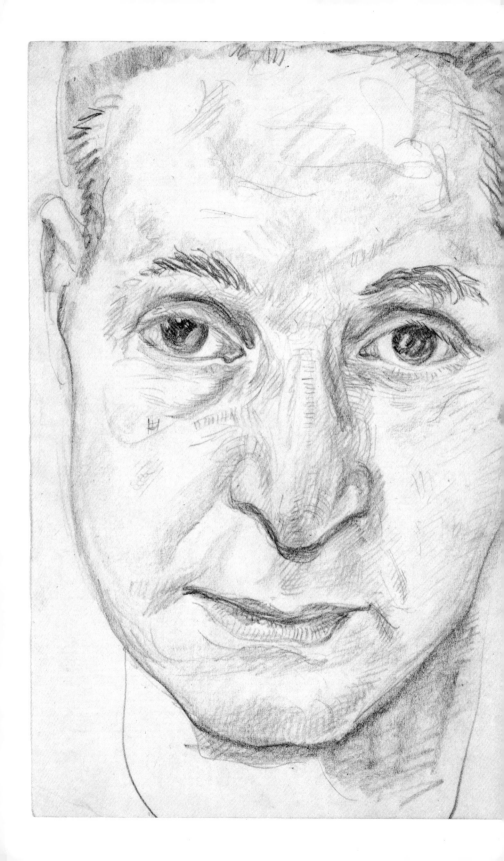

Bastard in the Ragged Suit

Writings of, with drawings by

HERMAN SPECTOR

Compiled, edited
and with an introduction by
BUD JOHNS and JUDITH S. CLANCY

SYNERGISTIC PRESS, San Francisco

Printed in the United States of America
by George Rice & Sons, Los Angeles
Text set in Times Roman by Hansen & Associates
Printed on 80 lb. Mohawk Superfine Text
and bound in Kivar by Sebco
Designed by Joseph M. Roter, with J. Clancy

First Edition

Library of Congress Cataloging in Publication Data

Spector, Herman
    Bastard in the ragged suit.

    I. Title
PS3537.P414B3   818'.5'208   76-17183
ISBN 0-912184-03-5

Table of Contents

WORK PREVIOUSLY UNPUBLISHED

Changed; In the Nickelodeon; The Bronx; Old Folks at Home; A Childhood Memory; Remembering His Mother; The Party Will Call Back; Remembrance of Childhood; Pop, Did Ya Bring Home Zymole Trokeys?; Fragment of Family Memory; Benny's Funeral; A Personal Revelation; Artist Into Stone.

.

Bastard
in the
Ragged Suit

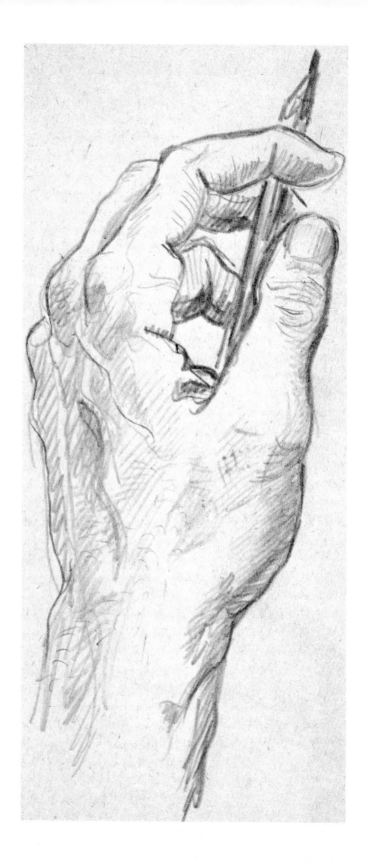

INTRODUCTION

Introduction

"1929 and a decade audible in these poems. The poetry tells this story, the tones of the poetry, even the borrowed tones, which are dreams, tell the story of a man who risked himself for the hope of a poetry that would isolate no man and no thing, that would seem to him in no way 'privileged' and he became perhaps the loneliest of the impoverished men of his time and I believe he must have become afraid. Before he died, fear had abolished the poetry."

George Oppen never met Herman Spector but he knew his work and, as the lines above establish, he also knew the man.

The words beneath a photograph of a youthful Spector in the February 1931 issue of *New Masses* can serve as a biographical starting point. Dressed in a suit with white shirt and striped tie, hair parted in the middle, he was not wearing the glasses through which Albert Halper remembered him peering "cynically, beseechingly, hungrily, and with pride."

"Herman Spector—Born 1905 in New York City and has never been farther west than 10th Avenue. Left high school after three years, the loser in a passionate struggle for a vital education, to fulfill the prediction of a pedagogue: 'You'll turn out to be a ditchdigger or a Bolshevik.' Worked, towards this end, as lumber handler, shipping clerk, truck driver, streetcar conductor, laborer, baker's helper, Western Union 'mutt,' factory hand, butcher boy, envelope addresser, canvasser, soda jerker. Now married, father of a 3-year-old girl, and engaged in writing a novel. Contributed to *Exile*, *The American Caravan*, *Free Verse*, *Anthology of Revolutionary Poetry*, *Transition*, *Unrest*, etc. Contributing editor of *New Masses*. Member of the John Reed Club."

Spector's contribution to that issue was titled "Unemployed." Later issues the same year carried "Cash or Credit" (March), "Those Ungrateful Masses" (September), "2nd Avenue Sweat" (in October when he was mentioned on the magazine's cover and the contributors' notes commented

"Herman Spector—has just lost his job in a warehouse. Looking for work.") and "Harlem River" (December).

From the time he first appeared in its pages with "Anarchist Nightsong" in June 1928, *New Masses* was the major outlet for the published work of the cynical youth who rejected his family's belt manufacturing business to become what Kenneth Rexroth has described as one of the major (and certainly one of the most forgotten) influences on the then-radical writers who came out of the period.[1] By that November, when *New Masses* carried four of his poems, his work had enough impact to warrant his name being on the magazine's cover and the following March he was first listed as a contributing editor, replacing Upton Sinclair in the alphabetical listing.

Edward Newhouse remembers him coming to the magazine's office now and then between 1929 and 1933, sometimes with Joseph Vogel, "whom I seem to remember as his good friend. He was a slender young man, of medium height, full of nervous energy; in manner, friendly, gay, sardonic."

"He was a very talented poet whom I knew for at least a decade," Vogel recalls. They first met in late 1927 or early the following year, probably through Horace Gregory and/or *The Second American Caravan*, to which both Spector and Vogel contributed.

"Spector and I used to get together from time to time, usually after working hours, to take walks in different parts of Manhattan and occasionally to attend an evening lecture. I recall our going to hear Sergei Eisenstein, and at another time Sidney Hook . . . I can't recall our conversations after all these years—the usual things young writers discussed, except our own writing. It seems odd now, but we rarely discussed our own literary work except to inquire how work in progress was making out. Naturally we both followed the little mags in which so much of our work appeared.

"Spector was tall and lean; he had penetrating eyes. One thing I admired about him, he could immediately see through sham. He had a devastating way of cutting through another writer's work in a sentence or two. He would even

---

[1]"It was a lean season for American poetry," Rexroth wrote in *American Poetry in the Twentieth Century* (Herder and Herder, 1971) of the literary generation made up of people born in the early years of the century who came to maturity in the troubled times after 1929. "Hundreds of young intellectuals who started out as writers were consumed and cast aside by the Communist Party. Most of them became political activists and gave up writing. The strong-willed ones obeyed the Party Line and dutifully wrote Proletarian literature and Socialist Realism. The stultifying effects of bureaucratic control are more than conclusively shown by the fact that all this passionate activity and commitment produced, in poetry, almost nothing of enduring value. America's revolutionary poets, Socialist and anarchist, flourished mostly in the old, free Radical movement before 1927, the year of Stalin's seizure of power, and those that came after belonged to dissident groups, mostly Trotskyites. Herman Spector, Sol Funaroff, Joseph Caylor (sic), Edwin Rolfe, are probably the best out of hundreds. Kenneth Fearing was always independent and suspect, and Kenneth Patchen, the best of all the poets of the Left of those days, soon became so, and Patchen, of whom more later, is the only one who is still read."

cut through the writer himself when an encounter took place. I recall we once met a young poet on the subway, and after a brief exchange of words Spector thrust a verbal knife right through him. My heart bled for the guy but I didn't say anything about my feelings to Herman. I never corrected his manners, he never corrected mine.

"In those days Spector had a job as collector of overdue payments for a furniture house, a job he detested. He used to tell me about the jerks he had to work with and for, and then listened sympathetically while I unburdened my own work gripes.

"It's impossible for me to recall now when we started talking about putting out our own little magazine. There was a lot of discussion about that, then more writers were drawn into it and to the naming of the magazine. The title *Dynamo* was finally decided upon. By that time the co-editors were Sol Funaroff, Spector, Nicholas Wirth, myself. We had numerous meetings to read manuscripts. Our original plan was to publish prose and poetry, but the submitted prose was so far below our standards that finally *Dynamo* appeared as a poetry magazine, mainly under Funaroff's editorship. When I sent a copy of *Dynamo* to my friend Edward Root (who lived at Hamilton College and later became famous as a talent scout in the arts), he astonished me by praising just one poem in the entire issue, the one by Herman Spector."

The first issue, *Dynamo '33*, was advertised in the January issue of *New Masses* as "a quarterly of proletarian literature" edited by Spector, Alexander Godin, Funaroff, Vogel and Wirth. That was apparently the issue in which the Spector poem praised by Root appeared and unfortunately no known copy survives. Vol. 1, No. 1 was dated January 1934 and three issues—the third carrying a review by Spector—appeared that year with he, Funaroff, Vogel and Wirth listed as editors. One issue of Volume 2 appeared the following Spring with the editor listed as "Stephen Foster," a name Rexroth says indicated that a Communist Party functionary had taken over the editing. It was the magazine's last issue.

Halper, who considered Spector "a rare talent, a rare person," wrote the editors of this volume that "his was an original talent, and his work deserves to be known today. A damn shame he never received the proper recognition he deserved during his life time." The two men first met through Vogel when *Dynamo* was being planned.

"*Dynamo* was born in my apartment, on 125th Street, in Harlem, one evening, with Herman, Vogel, Sol Funaroff and Alexander Godin present, in late 1932, as I recall. I had sold two stories to Mencken for his *American Mercury* and consequently was the only person present who had any money that night. I tossed in $25, and so *Dynamo* was born. I pulled out later, for personal reasons, and asked that my name be stricken from the masthead. But I saw Vogel, Godin and Spector on a friendly basis after that. I believe Kenneth Fearing came into the *Dynamo* orbit afterwards."

5

Both Spector and Vogel were mentioned by Ezra Pound in his February 1, 1929 letter of advice to Charles Henri Ford. Ford was about to begin *Blues* ("out of a blue sky, a magazine of new rhythms," promised an introductory advertisement that summer in *transition*) which included Spector and Vogel among its contributing editors, along with Eugene Jolas, Oliver Jenkins, William Carlos Williams and Jacques le Clercq.

"As you don't live in same town with yr. start contribs, you can not have fortnightly meeting and rag each other," Pound commented. "Best substitute is to use circular letters. For example write something (or use this note of mine), add your comments, send it on to Vogel, have him show it to Spector, and then send it to Bill Wms. each adding his blasts or blesses or comment of whatever-damn natr. Etc. When it has gone the rounds, you can send it back here."

Pound had told Ford "every generation or group must write its own literary program. The way to do it is by circular letter to your ten chief allies. Find out the two or three points you agree on (if any) and issue them as program. . . ." He did urge the magazine's support for his own program, including passage of some "decent and civilized copyright act" and amendment of Article 211 of the Penal Code with the 12 words "This statute does not apply to works of literary and scientific merits."

The letter to Ford continued: "You shd. look into Art. 211 and the copyright mess. If you don't want to attend to that part of the mag, get Vogel or Spector or some of the huskier and more publicke minded members to do the blasting."

Blues, which survived for nine issues, was introduced as a magazine "of a more complete revolt against the cliche and commonplace, welcoming poetry and prose radical in form, subject or treatment." Its editors considered it "a haven for the unorthodox in America and for those writers living abroad who, though writing in English, have decided that America and American environment are not hospitable to creative work."

Before the first issue of *Blues* appeared, Pound wrote: "If it is any use, I shd. be inclined not to make an effort to bring out another *Xile* until one has seen whether *Blues* can do the job. Or do you consider this excessive on my part? I don't see that there is room or need for two mags doing experimental stuff . . . at present moment." He lent further encouragement with "Seems to me a chance for the best thing since *The Little Review* and certainly the best thing done in America without European help."

Pound, who had published Spector's brief prose piece "Cloaks and Suits" in the Spring 1928 issue of *Exile*, corresponded considerably with Herman during the period which followed but unfortunately none of his letters to the young writer were saved. In 1973 Louis Zukofsky confirmed tersely that he was responsible for Spector's first publication in *Exile*: "Yes, I was. Can't say more."

Spector's name was still on the title page of *Blues'* eighth number (Spring 1930) as a contributing editor but Vogel's had disappeared and Herman's was also missing from the final issue that Fall. The political infighting of the Communist world was leaving its imprint on the writers of the Left, their publications and their personal associations.

The October 1929 issue of *New Masses* had carried a blistering letter by Vogel to Mike Gold under the caption "Literary Graveyards." It condemned the "evil influence on young writers" of *transition*. Vogel said the matter went back farther, to Pound.

"Ezra, it seems, is as incapable of good influence as the Church. Recently he tried to organize a group of writers in this country, but the only success—or harm—he achieved was the taking of a smaller Pound under his wings, namely Louis Zukofsky. Others of the group, including Spector, Moore, Gould, myself, somehow didn't grab the rope.

"One of the droppings Pound left behind is *transition*," Vogel continued, "And the harm *transition* has done is evidenced in a contagion about to spread in this country in the form of a crop of new magazines, which will appear in the near future. *Blues* appeared months ago, a washy imitation of its mama in Paris."

Vogel added that "*transition* and *Blues* continue with experimentalism that is old, that repeats, that becomes weaker and weaker, that serves little purpose . . ." and concluded by urging "it is time that young writers disassociate themselves from all these abstractions, as many have long ago done from Pound, the dean of corpses that promenade in graveyards."

The final issue of *Blues* carried, under "Contemporary Reviews," notice of the indefinite suspension of *transition*—"valuable organ of the innovative element in literature"—and a sharp blast at *New Masses*: "It would be a document of no little interest—that prepared by some studious psychologist, exposing the exact motives leading a large number of literary people to sentimentally unite their talents under such a title. Truly enough, since the title has been changed from *The Masses*, literary people have been inclined to drop off and non-literary people come on: Mr. Gold has had his particular vision. But God knows, the sins of print seem riotous as one peruses a copy of this periodical; the assumption being intelligibility, privilege of value, and literature, one accords only the first and that, one has to assert, is accidental."

Before he disassociated with *Blues* Spector had arranged for the first publication of a poem by Harry Roskolenkier (Raskolenko). They were friends as young men and while Spector had not been much inclined to carouse, when he did as often as not it was with Raskolenko.

"The bitterest man I ever knew, Spector was a poet who was published regularly," Raskolenko reminisced in *When I Was Last on Cherry Street*. "Ezra Pound, then extolling social-credit economics in Mussolini's Italy, had made Spector one of his faraway poet-protégés, and Spector made me his close-at-hand protégé. Spector was savage, brutal and brilliant, an innovator in poetry, and Pound admired his experiments. Spector came from the upper middle classes and loathed them. He could have been rich had he said yes to his father;[2] instead he took shoddy jobs to aggravate the cosmic hatred in his poetry. . . . Between his joyless poems and his misery-seeking jobs, he wrote explosive class-complaints to poets and editors."

Although harsh to a fault in his personal criticisms of Spector ("Though frightened of women, he married too early—and remained frightened, rudely unawakened to any job.") Roskolenko did partially understand that despite the economic choice Spector made because of his disdain for the middle class he never fit comfortably into the mold of the proletariat.

This by no means gave him what Joseph Kalar, in a 1929 call to *New Masses* for more creative writing, scorned as "the drawingroom scent of a Floyd Dell."

"The proletarian writers I particularly have in mind at this time are Ed. Falkowski and Martin Russak and Herman Spector: sufficient proof, I think, that a proletarian can write. . . ." Kalar said. "Let us keep *New Masses* open for experiment—there is room in it both for Herman Spector and H. H. Lewis, room, that is, both for the fine experimental work of Spector and the more traditional work of H. H. Lewis."

Five poems by Spector are known to have been in the Autumn 1927 issue of *Free Verse*, of which no known copy exists. One of them was certainly the poem included the next year in *The Second American Caravan*. "Nightowl" was published in the January 1928 issue of *Bozart*. Spector was 22 and before the year was over six publications would carry a total of 18 pieces reprinted in this volume.

His widow, Clara, recalls that Spector had published already by the time they met in late 1925 or early 1926 and that he showed her his work in print between then and their marriage in 1927. She doesn't remember where it appeared or what were the themes except for one that was certainly an exception to his pattern of "always tearing something down, he was sort of bitter about everything." That exception came after she told him about her grade school graduation.

"He took what I told him and he wrote it into a little story of this very young girl on her graduation day. He made a beautiful little story out of it that was published somewhere. That's the first memory I have of him getting some money (for writing). I think they gave him $15."

One of the little magazines which carried Spector's poetry in 1928 was *Palo Verde*. It was edited by Norman Macleod during a period when he was

[2]Questionable since the father, after a period of pre-1929 prosperity, was not a wealthy man when he died in 1956. Portions of Spector's previously unpublished "All the Speeches of the Presidents" deal with this.

custodian of the Petrified Forest National Monument in Arizona as well as a contributor to *New Masses*.

"I was writing very conventional, rather poor, imitative verse at the time," recalls Macleod, who is still active as a literary magazine editor with *Pembroke Magazine*. "It was Herman Spector and also Parker Tyler who wrote me advising me to climb out of that rut and so it was they who first influenced me in the direction of experiment and in trying to find my own voice and new forms—or at least to say what I was trying to say in language that was not distorted by restrictive English metrical patterns."

In January 1931 Macleod went to New York at the invitation of Walt Carmon, managing editor of *New Masses*, and became his editorial assistant. It was during this time he first met Spector, although he didn't see much of him. Carmon decided to take a vacation soon after Macleod's arrival "and left it to me to bring out the March 1931 issue.

"This was the number that published Whittaker Chambers' famous short story 'Can You Hear Their Voices?' (my title). I also published one of my own on the inside front cover of that issue. I selected the material[3] that was included and I did the layout."

Macleod was the American editor of *Front* (published in The Hague) that same year when it published "Bum's Rush," a short story by Spector. Both men were also among the *New Masses* poets who had work selected about the same time for translation into the French to be published in *Poèmes D'Ouvriers Americains*, a small anthology "brought out by probably the communists in Paris."

"I liked him and admired him," Macleod wrote in 1973 of Spector. "But he was uneven. The best of his work was quite brilliant."

Others had said that in print during the early Thirties. Alfred Kreymborg's *Our Singing Strength, An Outline of American Poetry (1620-1930)* listed "newcomers and poets of to-morrow" in its chapter "Youth Moves on Toward Maturity." ". . . one may advise the reader not to lose sight of Howard Baker, Stanley Burnshaw, Clarence E. Cason, David Carter, Malcolm Cowley, Martin Feinstein, Lincoln Fitzell, Horace Gregory, Eugene Jolas, Edwin Morgan, Cary Ross, Jay G. Sigmund, Herman Spector, Charles Wagner and others."

"In addition to Gold's contributions, important work has appeared in *The New Masses* from the pens of Joseph Freeman, Whittaker Chambers, Paul Peters, Langston Hughes, A. McGill, Joshua Kunitz, and Herman Spector," V. F. Calverton wrote in *The Liberation of American Literature*, published in 1932 by Charles Scribner's Sons.

"Our paths never crossed," wrote Carl Rakosi to the editors of this collection. "My only memory, not of Spector but of his poetry, is the thought at the time that he was trying to do the impossible, write Marxist poetry, and

[3]Spector's "Cash or Credit" among it.

that he might make it, but I don't remember any poem of his that did make it. He was making such a valiant effort and his work was so much better than that of others in *New Masses* that it looked as if he might succeed if he kept at it long enough."

In 1933 a 64-page book was printed by the Liberal Press, priced at 35 cents or $1 for one of the "125 copies of a specially bound limited edition." Not an earth-shaking event but it had impact . . . as described by Isidor Schneider in *The New Republic*:

"For Americans the publishing of *We Gather Strength* is an event worth dating. Here are four young writers who are building their careers as poets outside the capitalist publishing apparatus . . . The struggling left-wing literary magazines have provided them their public . . . They are not only creating a revolutionary poetry but gathering together what will probably be the most responsible and satisfying audience poetry can hope for in our time. We can look forward to something more from their joined strength than from any other group in America. . . ."

The four were Herman Spector, Joseph Kalar, Edwin Rolfe and Sol Funaroff.

"These are four young poets," wrote Michael Gold in his introduction. "They are hungry proletarians. Their minds are filled with images of death. They alternate between deathly despair and the wild wonderful dream of our World Revolution. Nothing is clear about them yet, except that they are actors in a great drama.

"Reader, this little booklet of poetry, and other books and pamphlets like it, are to be cherished and saved for the libraries of the revolutionary future."

Mike Gold, editor of *New Masses*, said the four "are keeping alive a precious spirit in our revolutionary movement which all the vulgarizers of historic materialism will never kill.

"I have always felt a peculiar kinship with Herman Spector. Bitter and lonely, the 'bastard in a ragged suit,' this poet of youthful revolt roams our familiar New York streets at midnight. He is the raw material of New York Communism.

"Confused, anarchic, sensitive, 'at times the timid Christ,' nauseated by the day's ugly and meaningless work, he prays for quick death to fall on this monstrous capitalist city. Then,

'a big Mack rolling and rumbling down the street
and lo! morning.'

"It is with such deeply felt metropolitan images and symbols that this proletarian poet builds."

Gold wrote of the other three . . . the ardor of Kalar, a young lumber worker and paper mill mechanic from Minnesota who had "power in him that has not yet found words"; Funaroff, "eclectic, derivative and rhetorical, jazz and revolution mix"; Rolfe, "spectator, he is critic; his judgments are cool and accurate, whereas in Kalar and Spector the class war goes on in every heartbeat and vein: they are torn by it, confused, passionate, real, the thing-in-itself."

The next year, writing in *New Masses*, Schneider said "Gold's collection of revolutionary verse and *We Gather Strength* have stimulated poetry to a new and fruitful subject matter and given to the revolutionary movement the beginnings of a rousing campaign music."

Nelson Algren recalls how he was so influenced by reading *We Gather Strength* that he memorized its contents and made his first trip to New York from Chicago to meet Spector and Funaroff. There he was flattered to learn that they were familiar with his work and, at a party, he heard a recording one of them—probably Funaroff—had made reading some of that work. The three marched together on Fifth Avenue with the Abraham Lincoln Brigade in a May Day parade, Algren pushing Spector's younger daughter in a baby carriage.

Despite the enthusiasm of Schneider, Gold and others for the future of *We Gather Strength* and its poets, the memory dimmed.

"The poets who appeared in *We Gather Strength* have worn less well (than Fearing and Patchen)," Allen Guttman wrote in his poetry chapter for *Proletarian Writers of the Thirties*, published in 1968.

"But when their collection was published Herman Spector and Joseph Kalar were greeted as the heralds of a new era in poetry, and their poems were treated as a bountiful harvest. Spector, whom Michael Gold characterized as 'the raw material of New York Communism,' seemed a proletarian version of the Man with a Hoe: 'I am the bastard in the ragged suit/who spits, with bitterness and malice to all.' Kalar . . . shared Spector's bluntness."

Guttman referred to Spector and Kalar being included, with 27 other poets, in Granville Hicks' important anthology, *Proletarian Literature in the United States*, but he felt the best poems in that 1935 volume were by Horace Gregory and Muriel Rukeyser, "two poets whose careers, like those of Fearing and Patchen, transcended the radical movement."[4]

The appearance of Volume 1, Number 1 of *Dynamo* led Waldo Tell to describe it in the February-March 1934 issue of *Partisan Review* as "the best collection of revolutionary poetry which has appeared since the publication of *We Gather Strength*.

[4]*A History of American Poetry, 1900-1940*, published in 1942, briefly credits *We Gather Strength* for holding the promise of a left movement in poetry, mentions *Dynamo* and calls the 1935 publication of *Proletarian Literature in the United States* (containing Spector's "Timeclock") the height of a phenomenon which "created great local excitement." But, after commenting that despite his death in 1942 Funaroff "was more fortunate than most young writers who shared his promise, his political convictions, and his poverty," the writers—Horace Gregory and Marya Zaturenska—quickly turned "with a sense of great relief" to Fearing.

"Not only have its editors (including Spector and Funaroff) collected in its 24 small pages some extremely significant literary contributions; they have also, as these very contributions reveal, set a high standard of literary merit which is sorely needed in revolutionary literature. It is a standard which proves that revolutionary literature—or, more precisely, in the case of *Dynamo*, revolutionary poetry—has definitely passed its hit-and-miss, catch-as-catch can period."

A 1935 article on poetry by Rolfe described both *Partisan Review* and *Dynamo* as being edited aesthetically as well as politically on solid, valid principles.

Soon after the publication of *We Gather Strength* Spector, who was living in the Bronx, spent two weeks (May 14-26, 1933) at Yaddo, the Saratoga Springs writers' and artists' retreat conceived by Katrina Trask Peabody and her first husband, Spencer Trask, for their 500-acre estate with its 50-room manor house.

"He loved it," Spector's widow recalls of Yaddo, which she thinks he also visited a second time. "He wished he could have stayed there."

Vogel had a somewhat more detailed memory: "I proposed Spector's name to Elizabeth Ames and she invited him to Yaddo. He was able to do some writing there, but his pleasure was a mixed one, he told me after his return, because a certain novelist had taunted him constantly as a proletarian rebel living in the lap of Wall Street luxury. It surprised me that Spector hadn't exercised his usual swordsmanship to cut down the bourgeois braggart; however, Spector hadn't wanted to create a scene, not at Yaddo."

No records are kept at Yaddo of what guests work on while there but others present during Spector's 1933 stay were Louis Adamic, Loyd Collins, Jr., Leo Fischer, Albert Halper, Charles Harrison, Grace Lumpkin, Evelyn Scott, John Metcalfe, Ferner Nuhn, Philip Reisman, Mrs. Reisman, Tess Slesinger and Carl Wuermer.

Ironically, *We Gather Strength*, *Dynamo*, Yaddo, the praise, were happening at the same time Spector began his withdrawal as an actively publishing writer. Politics, family difficulties, his own bitterness . . . all played a part but what weight for each, and what other factors were involved, nobody will know.

"We lived in the East Bronx," Alfred Hayes recalls in a letter about the period. "We belonged to the John Reed Club. We were all poor. Herman seemed poorer. He behaved poorer. And bitterer. And more saturnine. We were all bitter and all somewhat saturnine. He was just more. He had a wife and a child, and then there was another child. He looked like a man the universe had gone out of its way to trap. He worked somewhere. A factory? An office? I don't remember exactly. He was somewhat older than I was and I don't think he liked me and I was always somewhat uneasy with him. We were all thin and dark, but he was thinner and darker. He was suffocating. He couldn't leave his wife. He couldn't abandon his child, or children. He couldn't seem to break loose of anything, wife, children, Bronx, poverty, bitterness, thinness, darkness, anything. He wrote the kind of poetry Louis Zukofsky and a queer gent like Eli Something wrote: thin, emaciated poetry. I can't even remember the East Bronx anymore except for the streetlights. And a few Friday nights. . . ."

New Masses changed its approach—and its frequency, from monthly to weekly—in 1934, and Spector no longer wrote for it. Literary magazines virtually disappeared as the depression deepened and, as Rexroth contends, the Communist Party decided they no longer had an important function in its program. *Sweet Like Salvation*, which might have been either the novel or book of verse mentioned in biographical notes, had been announced but apparently never published. Spector was certainly not the kind of writer welcomed by *The Saturday Evening Post* and other successful mass magazines of the period, although he did make sporadic stabs at writing for them and the pulps as it got more difficult to meet his family's needs. But mainly he wrote, rewrote and didn't submit.

Then, about 1938, came a brief detour from the road he was traveling. He spent about a year on the WPA Writers' Project, working on its Living Lore project and actually earning a living as a writer.

"The writers went around the city interviewing people—without tape recorders—put down what they heard. More exactly: put down what they heard as strained through their particular way of recording it," recalls Saul Levitt. "And Herman's was among the very best of this stuff. . . ."

That's not surprising. He was doing what he liked and what he did well . . . and the project paid $25 a week.

"My own impressions of Herman and of his work are distant but quite vivid," Levitt continued in a 1973 letter. "Herman was lean, dark, nervous, despairing and funny. His poetry hit like electric stabs—I remember short stabbing lines—nervous style and urban words—dark sounds—staccato beat.

"He did one of his folklore pieces about a party of people in a taxi which loses its way to a cemetery. They either never get to the funeral or get there too late. An extremely funny piece but with that melancholy edge which made it Herman's. His dark side and his humor in some taut arrangement inside him like two hands in Indian wrestling.

"But I think, unhappily, it was the darkness which won out—accounted for Herman disappearing suddenly out of the world of poets and writers with whom he'd been associated—surrendering to some call back to what was masochistically secure—Brooklyn, driving a taxi, living lower middle-class, raising his children—griping. I don't make any judgment on his choice. It was his life's necessity to choose to do this. Which sets up many lines of thought I'm not going into in a letter."

The project did end and so did the detour. Spector didn't stop writing but, as Norman Macleod speculated years later, "at least he stopped sending it out for publication."

"Every night, every moment he had he turned to his writing," his widow recalls, adding that she didn't know what he was writing. "Until he turned to drawing and he stopped writing for some years . . . He wrote in longhand until later years when his sister gave him a typewriter for one of his birthdays. She was the only sister with money. She gave it with a note that she hoped he would create. This was years later (probably the early '40s)."

World War II came, and with it employment as a welder at the Brooklyn Navy Yard.

"At the time, I didn't think anything could unsettle Herman's indifference—seeming indifference anyway—to everything and everyone about him," Henry Gilfond wrote recently to one of Spector's daughters, both of whom he had taught in a Bronx elementary school.

"It seemed to me, again at that time, that he had given up on much and had become rather cynical. I may have been mistaken. His cynicism may have been a facade to conceal his inner turmoil (not lessened by the domestic difficulties he mentioned briefly). I'm sorry I didn't get to know him better. We had appeared in the same magazines and I'm certain that, given the time, we should have discovered much we believed and held in common. But we didn't give it the time. . . ."

"The darkness," as Levitt called it, continued to win out. In 1945 Spector and his family moved to Brooklyn, to the upper flat of a three-story house on a tree-lined street. The job as a welder ended with the war and he spent several years as a sales canvasser . . . sometimes for a photo studio, sometimes selling pots and pans, sometimes in New York, sometimes roaming Southern states.

Disappearance from the world of poets and writers with whom he had associated had at least one interruption and then Spector could not bring himself to admit to Halper that he was writing but no longer submitting his work for publication.

"I last saw Herman in the Borough Hall section of Brooklyn," Halper recalls. "He told me he was selling photo coupons for a commercial photographer, soliciting sales for weddings, graduations, bar mitzvahs, etc. What a horrible job: he worked on a commission basis. He added that he had recently become a grandfather. When I asked if he was still writing, he drew himself up with pride and regarded me unflinchingly through his glasses.

" 'Halper, I haven't written a line in 18 years,' he said proudly, with an air of defiance. I've never forgotten that little meeting with him on Fulton Street; it was the last time I saw him."

Shortly after the encounter with Halper, about 1949 or 1950, Spector became a cabdriver. The writing continued except for the period when he turned to drawing, drawing with insight on whatever paper was available.

14

These were mainly pictures of the people around him . . . family, the few friends, but more often his fellow hackies, people on the street and those he saw in the all-night cafes where he paused for coffee. The drawings might well be called autobiographical, as were the last pieces of his writing. Some are printed here for the first time: fragments and sketches, some about his young manhood, others for a book he contemplated from his cabbie experiences.

But he never finished them, was never satisfied, never again before his death the day before his 54th birthday in September 1959, submitted his talent to the opinion of editors, critics and public.

Oppen wrote Spector's artist daughter: "Yes, I think your father stopped short, or was stopped . . . Yes, sure, his spirit failed (but) he did a great deal more than most men have."

Writing for this book, Oppen referred to a 1928 *New Masses* essay by Spector.

"Of *The Dial* as representative of the literary currents he wrote furiously: 'You have imagined an audience, the piece is secondary'. He had encountered another audience, haunted and jostled by another audience, in love and hatred of that audience, in fear of rejecting them, in fear of another claim, he rejected most of the powers of poetry but there lives in his work the poetry of distance, of a jostled solitude, the poetry of a decade that he feared or even knew would be lost, that he fought for and fought against, that he drowned in and lived in and which may be lost.

    " 'Dead me no deaths,
      Ceasar of sad words.'[5]"

BUD JOHNS
JUDITH S. CLANCY

The published work of Herman Spector collected here is presented essentially in the chronological order of its first publication, followed by previously unpublished manuscript fragments selected by the editors from those discovered after his death. In cases where published work appeared in more than one form and was included in *We Gather Strength* that volume's

---

[5]From "No Deathes Mattr" by Herman Spector, *Blues*, 1929.

style is used here. Spector's punctuation and spelling has been retained from manuscripts, with the notable exception of *bagel* which he consistently misspelled as *bagle*. Where manuscripts indicated that he had not decided between two or more possible words or phrases we have included the alternative in parenthesis or mentioned it in an Editors' Note. In some cases it was impossible to decipher a word in manuscript and such omissions are shown here by spacing such as   . It is ironic that one of the earliest poems reprinted here was also the last Spector piece publicly published prior to this volume . . . "Billiard Academy" appeared in the September 1928 issue of *New Masses*, again in *We Gather Strength* and lines from it were printed in the September 1963 issue of *Scientific American*, four years after his death.

The drawings, all by Spector, are published here for the first time. The frontispiece, half title and drawings on pages 18, 56, 110, 114, 116, 140, 144 and 174 are selfportraits. The right-handed Spector also often used his left hand as a "model."

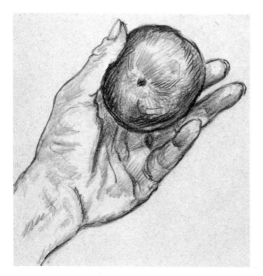

THE PUBLISHED WORK

NIGHT OWL IN A DECAYED HOUSE

there are snow and somewhat frost however
outside with the white streets and wind.
the clock tinnily interrupts tolling 2 or 3 times.
and the old man's snoring is a recurrent bur-zz.
here between ceiling and floor at the foot of the stairs
I pause,
reconsider suicide.
attenuated loneliness reaches for finality of death,
the patterns of life grow inept on the carpet.
today and now the clock ticks
the telephone is silent and hopeful
doors are slightly ajar.
tomorrow will certainly annoy me.
tomorrow will be somebody's wakeful cough in
        the still house;
spying on me, suspicious.
I will kill myself before I am eaten up
by the invidious stares of lepers.
a door opens on its hinge with a burglar's creak.
this house is rotten with evil
sweating with suspicions,
fear
and the wind drones, winds, blows outside.
the old man's snore is a violent complaint.
time for death.

Bozart, January 1928 (titled "Nightowl");
We Gather Strength; also titled "Today and Now"
in manuscript

CLOAKS AND SUITS

. . . Husky niggers run the elevators in
buildings where stinking specimens of inhuman-
ity with sharp, beady eyes and flushed faces
rush to and fro up and down and sneer
cigars. Badly painted girls and women in tight
pink camisoles walk about the floors casually
but that don't give nobody a Russian hurrah
because 1st they are used to it secondly a bad
sex to ye if ye think that Mr. Goldberger's
eye could ever wander from the tally-sheet
during business hours—or after. Mr. Gold-
berger is strictly business, except he goes to
see a fight once in a while or attends the open-
ing of some kind of teater where some kind
of a show is playing which never turns out as
dirty as you'd expect but Mr. Goldberger al-
ways tells what a hot time was had by all.
But Mr. Goldberger he usually don't have
much time for such tings his time is so pre-
occupied. All day long he is busy frowning at
salesmen and smiling at customers and bawling
out the help and in-between-times running in
and out of elevators trying not to look too im-
portant. You can't blame Mr. Goldberger for
sticking out his stomach in self-approbation.
The salesmen salaam and kiss his feet and vis-
iting buyers respect him because he got more
money than what they got and Mr. Goldberger
figures he could buy every dressmodel in the
building—if he wanted to . . . A jovial God
created Mr. Goldberger without teeth, and now
offers him nuts to crack.

Exile, Spring 1928

A POEM

blow moaning in the dark foggy morning,
    horn or something.
somebody's boat passes in water, swish-cut,
    and blows moaningly.
blows blows fainter, fades. 2 or 3. lets hope
    there's no collision, let's pity the poor
    sailorboys out at sea a night like this,
    or morning.
foggy continues horn. the waterfront is a
    place for dreams. silence interpolates
    ejaculation between moaned horns, and the
    earth sweats.
there is no peace on earth, nor goodwill
    among men, christ was a helluva liar,
    and water-rats may thrive or die in their
    homes among wharves.
the world is in a nervous sweat, awaits,
    expectant of some fearsome fate . . .
    rolling darkly, and the depths of turbid
    seas are aware of earth's unrest, and
    scathe, and wetly swell and swell . . .

blow moaning in the dark foggy morning,
    horn or something.

The Second American Caravan

(Editors' Note: *The Second American Caravan*, published in 1928, was described as "a yearbook of American literature." Edited by Alfred Kreymborg, Lewis Mumford and Paul Rosenfeld, it did not credit sources but Spector's first appearance in an anthology probably was reprinted from a 1927 issue of *Free Verse*. The 60 writers represented in the collection included Conrad Aiken, Sherwood Anderson, Nathan Asch, Kay Boyle, Hart Crane, Waldo Frank, Robert Frost, Katherine Anne Porter, Burton Rascoe, Mark Van Doren, Robert Penn Warren and William Carlos Williams.)

THREE POEMS

I

when Anna shall learn of my love
like the huge stereotyped night
and I have done with evasions,

then seven softly reasons shall flitter through
the cloudlike transparent content of her mind
and she will remug a gleaming visage
in the twisting concave convex mirror of time.

and she will open and her roots will feed.

II
TO SOMEONE REMEMBERED

when it is in the space of a body
the silence of a mind
when it is night on the earth

i will call for you,
i will cry
i will know you lost.

whenever on these rare occasions
i will be filled with the night,
i will call for you.

in the space of a body
the silence of a mind.

i will know you lost.
i will know earth last

who drinks my tears as rain.

24

A CURSE FOR MY
DEARLY BELOVED, DEARLY

may she forever die.
may she decay, calmly.
let this whorebody turn to dirt.
And I,
more than a spectator—
let me have peace, and surcease of love.
let no sobs shake me when I see
earth take her.

Palo Verde, Summer 1928

(Editors' Note: "Three Poems" appeared in the Summer 1928 issue of *Palo Verde*. In typescript under the title "From the Life" Spector grouped "Autumn Sensed Keenly," which appeared the next year in *Blues*, with "To Helen," which except for the change from Anna was identical to the poem above, and "To Someone Remembered," in that order.)

ANARCHIST NIGHTSONG

teardrop from my nose should show how cold the night.
6th Avenue L vertical prison-bars blackly compel me.
they move darkly into the past, intimate the future
with close ever-more-distant and precise conjunctions.
I drink the dark, press close to it with sexual ardor.
terror subtly underplays a vast and tragic symphony.
my sigh is gobbled whistlingly up by the wind.
the vague sharp outlines of grandeur point skyscrapers
against the inertia of black fog and nescience.
Union Square is now a dreary stark desert,
where evil lurks, seeps from the ground . . .
shines a pavement grin,
stares fixedly in sadist mania from out the subway signs.
strike down, O Lord of desolation and bleak murder
strangle this sick asleep chorus-girl city, smash,
press your thumb down lightly, smudge into nothing
the gross abomination of men's possessions—
answer the circumscribed and lightheaded jest—
return the facile sneer of men with interest—
kill the lousy bastards in their beds as graves!
wreck the damned machines to which all men are slaves!
let me know no more new york!
smashing, rending havoc be your work—
O Lord!
O Lord of loveliness and ugly death:
let all nights cease upon your last, chill breath!

New Masses, June 1928;
We Gather Strength

I BUY ONLY THE BEST

Taxiraincoats one dollar
Seventy-five.
All modish collegians wear em.
Proper pose is upturned brim,
Turndout glove, sleepy look.
Tie knot very small close to neck gentlemen.
Note boxcoat effect of lapels
Giving somewhat stentorian tone
To else soprano-like fancified habilimentations.
Sir kindly turn right a trifle:
   31 from crotch.
Observe please affectation of eccentricity
    direct from London
's smartest haberdashers wales and others
wear em. 2 95 why pay more.
Gents.
Damned if i know.

New Masses, July 1928

BEAUTIFUL BUT DUMB

THE KING OF SPAIN: A BOOK OF POEMS, by Maxwell Bodenheim.
Boni & Liveright.

The verse of Maxwell Bodenheim is competent, brilliant and pleasing to the ear. It rarely attains intensity because the words are tricky and often carelessly used, and tend to become meaningless. For this reason, a good deal of the imagery falls flat. His best stuff, nevertheless, is in the sensual vein. Bodenheim does not possess the vital intellect necessary to back up his aggressive pen. His affectation and nervously self-conscious sneers affect unfavorably the intrinsic qualities of particular poems. The bourgeois reviewers accuse him of being disgruntled and overly-sentimental, and they are right.

Ideologically Bodenheim is the perfect, vague "liberal" of indefinite intelligence. Like all the pseudo-intelligentsia and individualistic high school students, he is probably afraid of being "classified." But he possesses exceptional powers of analysis and description, and when not overcome by the specific "bee-you-ti-ful" weaknesses and diseases that he knows so well how to caricature, his poetry becomes very direct and very important.

New Masses, July 1928

WRITING A PIECE FOR THE DIAL

You picture the perfect academician as audience with raised eyebrows and sophisticated smile. You dream into being a weirdly phantastic dialect with content of no special character. Whom you call an "oeuvre". Sentences connectedly run from your fingers; you allow a lapse; a hiatus, an elipses here and there for further mystification, with subtle implications. You have imagined the audience; the piece is secondary. Like ringmaster Cabell, you stand on a fancified upturned barrel with upraised whip; your white horses prancing and performing their capers under compulsion to prolonged childish clapping. The applause gluts your soul and steels your ready hand, though a spectator or two deplores the cruelty or depreciates the merits of the performance. Those of little faith walk out throwing curses backwards, and alleviate their disgust at the nearest bawdy-house. Others watch, too lazy to object, too stupid to move, to question. But the majority is well-satisfied, and well-dressed with monocles, sit back with fat grins. These are the aestheticians, the self-conscious ostentatious intelligentsia of all nations. Their motto: "Pressed pants bespeak the cultured soul." It is to the company of these that the fiercely mustachioed ringmaster hies after every performance. They dribble out fond praises to him or reverently slap his back, or lewdly regard his eyes; he is a perfect Adolphe Menjou of the hour. This is yourself with cutaway dress-suit and boutonnierre. . . . You are all ready to receive the Dial award and enter respectable society.

New Masses, August 1928

TWO POEMS

i walk like a cat, i have its lust.
every word i say will be a word uttered in
      wretchedness and fury.
a cat is alive, and dies with pain;
      and wonder in its eyes, at the last.
i will be a cat; but i know, among men with derbies,
      with topcoats, with canes,
i will be outcast. . . .

deepening, coloring with magical softness
my all untearful melancholia
is hummed nighttime music,
and hopeless, sad refrains
of lovely, harassed poets.

stories are told of the waste of love,
and life—the tragedies endured
in silence, by the commonplace. . . .
but i am humming nighttime music,
and i am overcome by tunes. . . .

i too know wrenching, heavy agonies;
i never knew a happy day—
yet i live on, for magically softening
the bitter pains of circumstance
are strains of nighttime music,
and hopeless, sad refrains. . . .

JAPM, Sept. 17, 1928

B.A.
(Billiard Academy)

green tables spaced, alight
under yellowlow lights.
shirtsleeved young fellows pose
themselves in special attitudes
about them, stickinhand
or cigarette deftly
held, then slide cues
sharply through taut fingers. the balls
shine round and clear, quick blobs
of color on faultless fields,
where rapid vengeance rolls
and clicks, returns
or poorly judged, deflects
to pass and spend itself in motion
rebounding gingerly from cushions . . .
this play of pallid youths
reflects, in poolroom atmosphere,
psychology of waste.
grimly they twist
time into tangled skeins.
and pool-school students, lucubrate
the minutiae of nullities.

New Masses, September 1928; *Anthology
of Revolutionary Poetry*, 1929; *We Gather
Strength*; excerpts in *Scientific American*,
1963

SATURDAY EVE, EAST-SIDE

corner delancy and norfolk.
jazzband from the radiostore
plays majestically, inspiring
noble emotions;
plays softly, sentiment
ally . . weirdly, orientally.

a drift of fog comes from the north,
seeping through the electric landscape . . .

an elevated train at allen street
cuts across a lit chop-suey sign.

the pavements, being drizzled on,
shine diamondly in pebble-wise
under a hail of shifting lights . . .

earth has not forgotten its sadness;
and whores have eyes, like legs have knees,
from skirts, from faces.

within these urban angularities
and geometric patterns of despair,
the flowing lines of music trace emotion
in sinuous, vague curves through garbage-air

and a squat guy in a straw hat passing,
flips a stub of cigarette to the street . . .

New Masses, September 1928;
We Gather Strength

NIGHT IN NEW YORK

the city is a chaos;
confusion of stone and steel,
the spawn of anarchic capitalism.

it is night;
the clock in the square points the hour:
nine.

pornographic offerings,
eruptions on the skin of streets
from the tainted blood of commerce,
are electricly alight and lewd.

signs flash bargain messages.
with twinkling of legs, a slim whore passes,
turns a corner, disappears.
several remarkably interesting ideas
walk up and down the streets . . .
and the trolleys clatter.
taxis slide softly.
the blare of evening hurried movements
welcomes me, a friend, a customer.

whaddeyeread?—
telegram! journal! mail!
newspapers; blazoning forth with each edition,
news of the most momentous import;
their blatancy a sterile farce
in the subtle night.
the "el" trains rumble,
with a menacing undertone of hate.

and the city laughs rattlingly.
trolleys . . . clatter, back and forth.
taxis slide softly.
slick, suave limousines sneer, tooting horns.
a cop blows his shrill whistle . . .

all day in the shop and my back hurts,
my feet are like lead.
my stomach grumbles . . .
i belch.

the city is a chaos;
confusion of stone and steel,
the spawn of anarchic capitalism.

New Masses, October 1928;
We Gather Strength

SONG

what is good, is good in this world, despite city,
    despite bruise of the frail sensitive,
    despite autoblare, jazz, nightclubs, movies.

what is good, i see ever, men being poetic
    heroes among the mass, movement of life.

you will listen long to the city, a symphony
    by day and nightscenes, in sun and dark.
    low, melodic, spring-songs albeit stinking
    of money-lust . . . albeit local, closeby.

no fancy bigtime boulevardier now,
    alonewalking, through streets and streets
    the up-down jumbled places of a dream
    i say . . .

there is more than strikes the eye, strange perspectives
    (although i live nearby), the ever-recurring
    mystery of lascivious, twisting streets.
    sadness of forgotten places, and the incident

of neverfathomed humanity, living, being poetic,
    heroes, the mass itself, in movement, grand
    rhythmic in large measure,
    exquisite in small . . .

    twisting, torturing ever; alonewalkers.
    them as see things, them as feel, by day and
    nightscenes.
new-york is a grand town, symphony listened-to long . . .

New Masses, November 1928;
We Gather Strength

WANDERING JEW

let me look into the faces of coming-home-from-party janes &
    their guys.
let me peep into parks, where the black grass and bends is.
so late it is, I should be home asleep,
yet my bones itch with evening.
so I walk, I shall never be tired
and I shall never know rest:
but rather chilled, eager
neurotic in passion
endlessly walking . . .

and at last a blackness of death:
the glitter in my eyes shall cease.

New Masses, November 1928

P M SKETCHES

In automobiles fly guys ride, softly
slowly, along slum places
seeking a bit of the cheap exciting stuff.
A cold golden half of moon is in the sky.
some searchlight spots the dark from end to end.
This is the very west helldevil part of town
at the very worst, most sinister time.
I loll, and shoulder the stone, mouthing a butt.

TRUCK RIDE

At night, the smooth surface of streets, millions of precisely shining lights,
    a boozefighter sprawling . . .

Have you ever ridden atop a big truck going through a dead town at 2 a.m.?

Its lone buzz
a businesslike warmth
where all is cold and dead.

New Masses, November 1928

GROW UP, CHILDREN!

THE POET'S PROTEST, by Angelo de Luca, $1.50.
THE GRUB STREET BOOK OF VERSE, by Henry Harrison, $2

The Greenwich Village poets amuse themselves. They have good manners, they sip soup noiselessly, they are essentially virtuous. *The Grub Street Book of Verse* is an inspired collection of the sweetest, most inoffensive outpourings of the sweetest, most inoffensive poetasters in the country. Master de Luca, in calling the work *The Poet's Protest*, is kidding us. He registers his most valid protest in a little piece entitled, "To My Unworthy Critics." The poem preceding that, strange to relate, is called "Premonitions of Genius—A Bid for Immortality." In the words of this poet: "O fame, O life, O youth, repent, repent!" We think that is the best line in the book. The next-best is also very appropriate: "If you do not die too soon, you will grow up." Amen!

New Masses, December 1928

A SNOB'S POTBOILER

THE STAMMERING CENTURY, by Gilbert Seldes. John Day. $5.

You would never suspect it, but Gilbert Seldes is a friend of the masses —he says so himself. Only in an intellectual way, of course. Nothing stupidly political or fanatic. He defends them against the inconsequential Menckenian concept of "a special boob class" versus a few wisealecky little Menckens. To a good democrat like Gilbert Seldes, we are little boobs. Of course, "radicals" are more so than others. Radicals are people who suffer from an inferiority complex. All radicals are alike—pretty sick, all of them. Social radicals are persons who would like Capital and Labor to be friends (imagine! but he actually says it) which would make a pretty dull sort of world, thinks Seldes. Stale wisecracks like these for over four hundred pages and five dollars, by a Doctor of Outlines and hack writer for the *Dial*, *Saturday Evening Post*, and the *Herald Tribune*. Then, toward the close, Mr. Seldes lets us in on a secret. You know, he is something of a classicist, concerned with the higher things of the spirit—more or less pure "idea." You know what I mean. The kind of man who can say without blushing in an article called "Debunking the Debunkers" (Herald Tribune, Oct. 21, 1928): "Debunking has been useful, entertaining and financially successful; but as I suspect that it has been an inadequate, often silly, always superficial criticism of American life I have tried to discover in it the element of bunk which blunted its instruments." All very well, but a rather ambitious task for a liberal-classicist-individualist, who, hopelessly confused himself, tries dishonestly to confuse the reader by likening the Marxian communist to the amusing "cranks" of the nineteenth century. His great discovery, apparently, is that we are all boobs—and yet:

"There are, of course, superior human beings marked by independence. These, however, are not a class, but individuals, capable of resisting both the majority and the minority, untouched by suggestions, resisting or following the current *as they choose*." Such as Mr. Seldes, we are to assume. Therefore, he is not speaking for himself, but for those "in the rut," as he calls it. That's what it means to be a democrat! Contradictions like this are typical. After stating that "the ancient radical ideas are soft and ridiculous in the eyes of the communist, just as the old banners of democracy are trampled under the feet of Fascism," he goes on to describe the communist as an aberrated cultist, inferior in importance even to the puritans of sex and diet. The most "individualist" reader, thinking these matters out, will automatically reject such sophistry. It is written, we suspect for those bluff, hearty, prosperous, thoroughly normal democrats of the Saturday Evening Post clan.

Seldes gets modest in the introduction, called "A Note on Method." "My original idea was a timid protest against the arrogance of reformers in general." Then he says: "I came gradually to want to prove nothing." Gentle reader, he has gone and done that very thing, conclusively, and again and again.

New Masses, December 1928

LIBERALISM AND THE LITERARY ESOTERICS

This article has one sufficient purpose: to show why the farcical literateur, the psychotic dilettante, is received with so much applause and reverence by the "enlightened" sophisticates of modern bourgeois society;' and, incidentally, why those big sales on modernistic furniture go over so well in the department-stores. If this is the age of the freak in matters esthetic —and to judge by the work of our more successful modernist artists, it certainly is—then I believe the fact can be explained, sociologically. The explanation hinges upon the concepts of liberalism; the bourgeois substitute for a scientific education.

Why is it that the man of genius and the scientist, in past generations as well as our own, has had only contempt for the "liberal", as the term is currently applied? Why is it so easy for every half-educated and uninspired shopkeeper to warm up at once to the tenets of the liberal philosophy? What is responsible for the mass of cynico-sentimental, "rationalistic," nihilistic intelligentsia who float about the streets and theaters of New York, bursting with philosophical conversation and booze? Why is Maxwell Bodenheim? The number of literate persons in America must be very high, but we would like to find out what the hell they are literate about. America reads more books and wears more spectacles than any other country on the map, and in America the liberal tradition, in its vulgarized version, is strongest. By "vulgarized version" I mean merely applied liberalism, for the liberal philosophy has proven to be corrupt in essence, regardless of what important work has been done by the really brilliant men who have contributed to its original luster. These pioneers will be recognized and remembered for their merits, for they represented the best thought of a once revolutionary bourgeoisie, but the ideology they nurtured has proved a futile one.

What I am saying is by no means new to communist thought. We already know that the liberal is a fellow who professes to be beyond-good-and-evil, free from ordinary human prejudices, a man who assumes in himself the utmost objectivity, the "olympian detachment" about which we hear so much. We know that the liberal is a stand-patter (although obsessed with a vague notion of "progress"); an ascetic or nihilist in his attempted escape from earthly subjectivity; and all in all a very fragmentary sort of thinker with no motivating ideals for the correlation of literature with life. He is not a static thinker, his thought is fluid enough, he favors the theory of the Bergsonian flux, evolution, and freudian optimism. It is the classicist who is a static. The liberal is no classicist, he believes in an "advance," he may even favor radicalism for this very reason, though not because he has acquired a scientific bias. He pretends to no bias whatever. He ridicules everything, he is a cynic, and he soon deserts the pose of radicalism when it becomes too uncomfortable. He has little enough courage to follow any cause, he exalts his weaknesses and pathological traits as virtues (as, psychoanalysis), and he is really an anti-intellect, though his vulgarization of the term, intellectual, has brought it into bad repute. So we have in the liberal a coward, a pervert, and a nihilist. And to such a man, whose thought springs from roots of bourgeois cynicism and despair, the modern esoterics who pander to and exaggerate his own infirmities, possess an irresistible appeal. However, it would be pertinent, before going into the psychology of the "new art," to explain the part of the *intellectual* in the communist program.

Naturally, I am pro-intellect, as I believe every real communist is, for this is implied in the furtherment of life. If communism meant a denial of life and a vulgarization of the intellect, I would cease to be a communist. But it is the bourgeois cynic, the Greenwich Village type of parasite, who is fundamentally anti-life and anti-intellect. The communist looks upon the functionings of intelligence in the most natural and scientific light, and wants more of it. However, in the program of world-advancement and the overthrow of oppressive capitalist forces, two things should be carefully noted. First, the already-present vulgarization of words must be taken into account. Just now the word "intellectual" means very little and Lenin and Trotsky used the term with contempt, as signifying the Hamlet, the sentimentalist functioning *in vacuo*, the academic scholar, pedantic and corrupt. Neither Trotsky nor Lenin nor Marx had any contempt for the sincere processes of thought, they did not employ the term "scientific socialism" in vain. But if we are to call our newspaper columnists, novelists, fashionable poets and panderers of all sorts *intellectuals*, then we may discard the term with profit. *And speedily, it must be remembered, above all, that this civilization is made possible only through the productive efforts of the WORKER, and that this is going to be a WORKERS' WORLD*, wherein all will be workers, and thinkers. It is true that there shall be *compulsion* to work, and *encouragement* to think, but this is as it should be. Fundamentally this will be a world of equalized economic distribution, and the intellect which would play an authentic part at this stage of our culture must be social-minded and proletarian. That intellect which is still circumscribed and hampered by such concepts as "individualism," "liberalism," etc., can not hope to be able to interpret the life of today. For with all the good will in the world, we must recognize that education is a fact, and that writers who deal with life must know of the basis of that life, and take some position with regard to it. They can not function then as romantics except for the purpose of providing an idle hour's diversion, in the manner of the comic-strips. We usually think of literature and art as more than diversion. Certain innocuous kinds of poetry and the plastic arts, at times, may be decorative: for profound values received, however, we need the word *education*. No writer can educate us who is not educated politically, himself.

To return to the school of "new art," which embraces such famous esoterics as Gertrude Stein, James Joyce, E. E. Cummings, and the magazine Transition. They were born with the modern discovery of the Unconscious, an organ or entity for the mystification, obscuration, and sexualizing of all knowledge. They are each a variant of more or less talented cynic, nihilist, hedonist, associationist, naturalist, freudian, and dada-ist. The last is a very descriptive title. Our modernistic artist is determined to be as Unconscious as possible. And since Freud has had to go way back into childhood or further to uncover the cause of our delightfully interesting complexes, the esoteric tries to go as deeply into his chaotic and underground beginnings as he can, so that he may approximate a naturalistic Method. This Method is to be born of the union of literature with the Unconscious. It resembles somewhat Dreiser's attempt to marry surface-detail to literature in order to produce Realism. But the "naturalist" way is much simpler, inasmuch as even surface-details have to be remembered, and are therefore a great bother to the Unconscious types of genius who would rather let the Unconscious do all the work. Miss Stein may be taken as the prototype of the new school, since most of the others boastfully acknowledge their "great debt" to her for having taught them Method. Such are our credulous "intellectuals", that the editors of Transition say: whenever miss stein writes anything whatever we will take it and print it wherever and whenever we damn please, howsoever, and bejesus—or words to that effect, or non-effect. And then the Stein goes into a trance, and the thing is done. The esoterics who, by the way, have a sort of prejudice against arguing their cause, immediately talk about the "abstracting and the exploiting of the word" performed by the eminent witchdoctor, like a laying-on-of-hands. This is why, when it refers to such delicate matters of esthetics, I don't mind being taken for a rank reactionary by the "enlightened" crowd, who have in Joyce and Stein merely a new Jesus and Virgin Mary of immaculate-conception capabilities. However, in regard to the necessity for a definite break with the past and a greater intimacy with life in letters, I find myself in substantial agreement with them. Indeed it is my sincere belief that Transition is the most alive and important literary force in our transition civilization: it voices the beginnings of epical melodrama on earth, and is ready for great things. But the esoteric whose delight it is to astound the yokelry in Mencken fashion is merely serving the cynical bourgeois "liberal" tradition; and plays the role of the opportunist in art.

To get the record straight it should be clearly understood that James Joyce is a master artist, and Gertrude Stein an occasionally interesting one. Cummings, too, has a biting fine talent. It is the colloquial influence they exert and the general "esotericizing" trend of their Method-over-literature that we find so odious.

New Masses, January 1929

BLUE NIGHTS

winter comes on.
I in winter, always the russian,
        do enjoy myself.
my pop said to me when I was young:
in Russia, i as a boy, went sleighing
        into blue nights.
pop, there are blue nights here too.
blue nights of frost,
strange blue frozen evenings
and I do enjoy myself,
pop.
as though I were a Russian
boy; sleighing, sleighing.
nights of snow and the white tang
of empty snow.

New Masses, February 1929

SNAPSHOT

72 street travels the spaces of sadness
downtown, 2nd avenue, the jewesses gleam.
regular blocks in the bronx, up and down:
little toy places under high stars.

harlem: sleek negresses.   beauty-parlors.
riverside drive sneering through mist.
mundane, they walk in their flesh, these harlots,
they glisten and pique the sense.

ah under the el trains at allen street,
the bowery's last whiff of booze;
gasoline motors going
across the bridge into brooklyn,
under a glimmering moon.

in central park the lamps are languid;
dazed with the slow death of night,
its last lingering caress.

(the stone is smooth, hard: 2 a m,
and no-one moves.
coldly the wind comes, filling my nose,
bitterly blowing . . .
i drink and i sob and i stifle a yawn.

sleep.   and the noisy trolleys clatter.)
dawn will come, over the highest building,
with roseate light, with morning papers,
busy people, toothpick chewers;
street-cleaners.

Palo Verde, 1929

CRIME IS A BUSINESS

CHICAGO MAY, A HUMAN DOCUMENT, *by Herself*.
The Macaulay Co. $2.50

Chicago May was one of the crooks who are called crooks. The crooks who are not called crooks supplied her with large or small amounts of money, inadvertently, sometimes willingly, for the favors of her sex, and immunity from blackmail. Chicago May considers crime a business. The real interpolation is: Business is a crime. She knows the interiors of numerous prisons. She has witnessed the sufferings of the proletariat under capitalism: she leers at the preachers and philantropists and all the monocled liberals of the bourgeoise. She asks: "Is it any wonder crooks are crooks, under society as at present organized?" What she really means, but is either afraid or is not permitted to say, is: This society is organized by successful crooks who are jealous of their spoils and hound us little fry into an early grave. We labor for the "State" in prisons and die of lousy diseases, because we are outlawed guerrillas fighting an immense predatory system. We are too dumb to learn economics and the tactics of the class struggle, but oh, you lousy filth on top, how we detest you and how we wish we were in your place! We know there is something rotten in America, but we are futilitarians, we gotta live meanwhile, and we are too tired and harassed to think! *Chicago May* is valuable as record. Personally, the author exhibits a lively intelligence and was probably advised, by editor and publisher, to tone down on the "preaching." Yet from observations that do occasionally escape here, I conclude that Chicago May, one of the crooks who are called crooks, has radical opinions about society and the crooks who are not called crooks.

New Masses, February 1929

FANTASY: 1929

It was a National Safety Week, sponsored by the Society for Prevention of Cruelty to Poets. Religion was in a bad way: the church funds were being defecated. Signs in all the cars of every train in each subway-line read as usual:

> Spitting is Prohibited,
> being a Crime, or $500,
> or BOTH!

There were newspapers, and where there were newspapers, there were journalists. Seven pimply virgins had committed crimes in a single week: the situation was Enormous. Two famous novelists, (married to each other), said that the main issue of the forthcoming election was prohibition. A professional jew had written a novel advertised to be "As TENSE and PATHETIC as an Erotic Dream." Freud was overwhelmed with remorse. A notorious broadway playwright announced that the communists had no money and no influence, whereupon five bookreviewers cheered. "Nation's Business" promised an american mussolini, and Dorothy Parker rhymed "zowie" with "-andhow." A manifesto depreciating the purity of public comfort stations was issued and signed by Wyndham Lewis, F. P. A., Wood Krutch, and Charley Chaplin. Highschool girls began to find Mencken an awful bore, realizing the infinitely greater wisdom of Valentino, who died on time. This kind of repetitious cynical bilge was probably discovered and patented in the times of Gilbert Seldes, god rest his weary soul, and later adapted and used with phenomenal success by Variety, Vanity Fair, The New Yorker, and The Commercial World.

 . . . The lights glow tenderly on fifth avenue, they sweat on broadway, they sneer and smirk on riverside drive. There are persons who prefer to read Books and go about thinking Art. Homosexuality attracts them; they are Liberal that way; they live in the Village for a thrill. Others drugged in a routine of work, productive or assinine, go to hear a blackface jew comic at the Hippodrome, with a glib tongue, enunciate nothing painfully. In the public libraries there are crowds of people trying to forget that they need a job, money, happiness; they have been taught to laugh at communists. Hunchback literati, sincere or careerist, they go from the Automat to Zero's Tub, talking Art: they have been taught to sneer at communists. A columnist in the World jocosely explains that animal good-health is making of him a "philistine" (hee, hee!)—having had a fairly adequate meal at the Algonquin, he observes that the rebels are envious. A reader replies: I spit upon your stale cautious phrases, you puerile academician, you . . . He weeps into the wastebasket, rebukes the correspondent for lacking a sense of humor.

Ohhh-h-h! the jazzmusic cries, dressmodels think the Boss is the nicest kind of man since he predicts greater prosperity for All, and a kid of 16 with gloating hopeful eyes works 13 hours a day for advancement: he has been taught to despise communists. If at first he dont succeed, he has been taught to try, try again. Thus doth virtue triumph, say the teachers of the land, who are virtuous, crabbed, and Loyal. And near times square a moving lighted sign announces: "Prince Matchiabelli Smokes Our Cigarettes!" . . . Suddenly: "And Who the Hell Are You?" it asks. The logic is indisputable. A white-haired philanthropist stands in the center of columbus circle and shouts to an audience of fairies, disappointed soda-jerkers, tired harlots from new england, crummy bums: "God is Love and money is Money; so don't confuse the two, or rather, the three!" The louder he shouts, the wider their mouths. It is late, late as hell; they are missing precious sleep; the white-haired philanthropist sleeps all day long; my, what pleasure he takes in trying to make these people as miserable as possible; he is not long for this earth; thank God. These thoughts, and others even less pertinent, assail them as they wait and listen undecidedly, but for a God which is Love but not MONEY they have nothing but scorn. Listless, they leave one by one; until at last, alone in the center of columbus circle, the spick, philanthropist, suddenly ceasing to smile, stumbles from the platform. . . . In central park the lamps are languid, dazed with the slow death of night, its last lingering caress . . . turning over and over, the sleeping phantom form of a lover, the park, involute paths and bends. . . . Once, in a dream, a man approached another man along a solemn silent street at night, and guided him up tenement steps to a room where a pink girl lay; pacific, placid, toothpick-chewing. He looked, and lo, it was good, and as it sayeth in the Bible, he went in and was surfeited. He walked outside; the streets were still, and pools of phlegm shone under lights; the stone was smooth, hard, 2 a. m., and no-one moved. Coldly the wind came, filled his nose, bitterly blowing: he drank and he sobbed and he stifled a yawn. . . . Rumor later reaching him to the effect that the panderer was her illegitimate son; he recalled with a shudder the ratty softspoken guy, the sad look in his eye. And her name was Mary. . . . So reads the sunday-morning paper, and it shows how an gorilla or orang-outang; it do not think; but We, We are M-E-N; we Think. Therefore we also see the estimable Mr. Brisbane, he writes a cartoon showing how some peop-le, they are Drunkards, and enjoy them-selves; but Good peop-le, they do not Enjoy themselves; they work for a Boss. Moral: Think, think; if at first you don't succeed, don't Drink yourself to Death or play Roulette at Mounty Carlo; but try, try again. And so, blithely remarked F. P. A. and Heywood Broun, two of our leading liberals, and So to Bed, each by each, and nicey nicey dreams. . . .

New Masses, February 1929

A POWERFUL STORY

THE CASE OF SERGEANT GRISCHA, by Arnold Zweig.
The Viking Press. $2.50.

Arnold Zweig has written a fine, realistic story of the war, using as factual material the true story of a Russian prisoner-of-war who escapes, is recaptured, taken for a spy, and executed—though everyone knows he is innocent. This is not a great novel simply because there is too much delicate Schnitzlerian insistence upon the individual psychology, while too little use is made of the flashlight of social intelligence. However, the cumulative effect of the book is one of powerful, stark tragedy. Zweig exhibits a great deal of brilliance in satirical chapters like that entitled: "Portrait of an Autocrat"; and certain incidental characters are successfully and vividly portrayed, though not always to the advantage of the novel as a whole. For example, the strict, mildly liberal general "of the old school," Von Lychow, only serves to sentimentalize and distort the significance of capitalist warfare. Persons like Babka, the faithful sweetheart of Grischa, and Tawje, a philosophical and fervent old Jewish carpenter, are true to life and add to the scope of the novel. But much of the day-to-day detail is irrelevant and tends to drag the action of the story. Too often we encounter the old familiar reiteration of mellow introspection, but despite these lapses, "Grischa" is full of meat; its theme and background alone recommend it; and it can honestly be described as "a darned good book."

New Masses, March 1929

REALISTIC SOVIET ART

THE NAKED YEAR, by Boris Pilnyak. *Payson and Clarke*, *$2.50*.

The Naked Year proves the case for contemporary Russian literature, and effectively lays the Propaganda-Ghost raised by excited liberals and weak Talents. . . . If any one in this democracy functions as strongly and successfully as an individualist artist as Boris Pilnyak does in Soviet Russia, I want to meet him. Done in the boldest of futurist technique, this story of the famine period in post-revolutionary Russia nevertheless establishes contact with reality at every point. It is a whirling, skidding kaleidoscope of people and events; pausing a moment here and there for complete absorption of a particular scene. Pilnyak is a master of poetic description in a direct, unemotional prose attack, and repeats, repeats; beginning again and again in a process poor Gertrude Stein foresaw, but could not successfully employ, as she was a little too much in love with the idea, narcistically, and forgot its purpose and end in creation. What is more, we get an accurate and brilliant dissection of the Russian mind, explicit and implicit, in a method employing movie "shots" and "throwbacks" and continuous merging of scene. This novel has the unity of a dynamic movie besides; it has the perfection of vital poetry, it is keen and unbiased. The story is Russia in transition, years of starvation and bloodshed, people in an age-old town awakening to the red dawn. The big thing to remember is this: Boris Pilnyak is unafraid; he leans neither forward nor backward because he has the balance and poise of a runner; he unbalances and affrights the detached, "contemplating" aesthetes of America. What a stink, we recall, was made over the novel *Sergeant Grischa*, recently published! It was a *masterpiece*, a *great novel of the war*—the journalist and high-hat critics pretended to be illuminated, profoundly moved. . . . Let us see how they meet this book, a grim and exquisite interpretation of real life as felt and historically viewed. . . . We predict in advance that the critics will have to resort to metaphysics, to sober discussions of "form."

New Masses, May 1929

YELLOW LAMPS

yellow lamps are manifest, are obvious.
yellow lamps are definite.

they are justso, as it grows night.
oh they are sure.

who gives a damn for dark
and deep, damp mysteries?

not yellow lamps,
sneering through rain,
leering at mist.

not yellow, proud lamps!

Blues, 1929

NO DEATHES MATTR

dead me no deaths,
ceasar of sad words.
obscure not the meaning of a lifes collapse
with obscene, vague nobleness.

death is a coldness.
dont get hot about it.
its an end.
dont begin on it.
dead me no deaths,
o sad pseudoteacher.

i eat,
i see,
i am going . . .

a train swallows space thru the tunnel
and at last wins the other end.

i wallow in dark caverns.
i shall come out into light.

Blues, 1929

A WOHMMN

i wann, i wann a wohmmn
whose touch hrts.

no mere alyin en allayin drab.
no cynico-mundane dust,
no haddit befaw . . .
i wann a wite wide wohmmn,
promising maww.

o, sing er softly under me now!
i know the banked caress,
the side-to-side weaving.
her womb is wide,
her flesh is swift with tenderness . . .

reech me in my agony!

tears r no damn good;
but things to eat r good.
a continually eaten wohmmn
with vast hungriness . . .

(on cool days, the streets are bare.
walking; her skirt blows
around firm legs.
the sun glos over er.)

Blues, 1929

FROM THE LIFE

To Clara

I'LL BE GODDAMNED

poison in my veins maybe tears and gall to my soul
pain head misery hard strain waste
i frown wretch look look grind kill
she too through weeps weeps weeps tears down
break break break down
why why why
this is what i mean when i say:
there is evil
there are evil people
there is evil.

blood-red, the leaf-things, and some are
    rust and green.
in solitude is autumn sensed most
    keenly.
there is nothing sad, none over the soil,
    none under, bewailing emptiness.
    this silence is glad; this death
    is profound.
when it rains, in spots for a second,
    when a crippled boy comes by,
    for a second there is a sob and
    a weeping.
then emptiness; a cool question.
    i want solitude keenly,
    scraping of leaves over walks,
    swishing: blood-red, or rust
    and green, and autumn most
    keenly, a question, profound.

P M SKETCHES

1

ah rain you so moist pavements
and foggily obscure lone lights
and smell me of the damp earth-air
i know its pleasure where the trees roots are

2

John Ward's sign makes melodrama on deserted street.
red-ghastly glow for a sidewalk's space
lets a lone bum pretend.

3

why acts become haunted at night,
no-one can say.
newsboys even harshlys message
gripes the dark like the death of a whore.

Blues, 1929

OUTCAST

I am the bastard in the ragged suit
who spits, with bitterness and malice to all.

needing the stimulus of crowds,
hatred engendered of coney-island faces,
pimps in a pressedwell parade,

I, looking into faces
(some say nothing; or with a leer—
see what the years have done to me,
and be confused,
unbroadway heel!)

at times the timid christ,
longing to speak . . .
women pass hurriedly, disdainfully by.
men, pigsnouted, puff
and puke at the stars . . .

recalling the verses of sensitive men
who have felt these things . . .
who have reacted, to all things on earth,
I am dissolved in unemotion.
won by a quiet content,
the philosophy of social man . . .
The high hat gods go down the aisles.
I am at one with life.

New Masses, March 1929;
We Gather Strength

URBANITE DELAPIDATE

friend, you are wearied,
as from no knowledges of death,
nor with ennui . . .
but sitting, never more than whistling things,
your face is softly tragic now; you seem
to have a certain solemn majesty
amid the flare of steel, whitepaint,
and passengers asquirm.

whence comes this sudden evening sadness, peace?
what brings the frightful frown to be forgot?
the venomed lust, now hidden, and a sheet
of unread morning paper on your lap . . .
your nodding head.
ah, you are tired.
wearied, not of life
nor from wise knowledges of death . . .

but the damn misery of flesh
awaiting loveliness:
the stark and neverfelt caress
of softness like the night

not knowledges of death.
nor consciousness of things forgot,
but simply, longings: tortured lusts,
that makes this business vulture's head to swim . . .
and gives him such a majesty
in sleep.

New Masses, March 1929;
We Gather Strength

THESE ARE THOSE BACK-AGAIN,
ONCE-BEFORE, HOME-AGAIN BLUES

omnipotence, abstract of the flesh
visualize
the time and place, eternal.

this corner, where i dangle like a fly
a space as mad and frightful once
feeding the brutes
alive as you and i.

came here where no concrete,
where no steel, electric was,
mans labor and mans brain
spent, the quiet lavatory,
the speeding train.

no bulb under moon in cool nights,
frosty, frosted, insulation assured.
but dank, but hoar-damp, in the dark
beasts nervously leering,

click-click: now the city!
now brilliant night silences!
cautiously planned streets:

around a corner, dangling like a fly,
nickelinslot adventures wait . . .
concrete, steel, electriclights . . .

Blues, 1929

VOICES

o them husky iridescent vaudeville voices
of chorine bimboes with avoirdepois
come out of the funnygraft or radiostore
with an i-wanna-wanna; dont-forget-me allure

o them gorgeous aggravatin vaudeville voices
they titillate and scintillate with lewd implications
oh wontcha ho-o-old me in your arms?
oh how i lo-o-oves ya, honeybunch!

melancholy mommas with quivering breasts
slowly twist in a tummy dance
oh ya go-o-otta know how, ya go-o-otta know how,
ya go-o-otta know ho-o-ow ta do it!

an if ya cant keep your ma-a-an at home,
dont ya cry-y-y when he's gone!

reciting plaintive, crooning tunes
out on the street cool afternoons
with throbbing throat and gestures lewd
describing arcs of lassitude—
sweet poppas languish by the store
in rapt attention, wait for more
and while the music grips their knees,
they writhe in lonesome lecheries—

oh them redundant anguished words
sung in a stagey, cracking voice
possess a false, perverted lure
like the firm plump legs of a chorus girl!—

and in their dreams, these old donjuans
caressing womens subtle charms
grow tender, brave, and bold; and hold
eternal beauty in their arms . . .

o them throaty coy hoarse imploring vaudeville voices
of chorine bimboes with avoirdepois
come out of the funnygraft or radiostore
with an i-wanna-wanna; dont-forget-me allure.

New Masses, May 1929

A VERY LITTLE INCIDENT

To you, nothing happened. But look you how big it is when I magnify or isolate it like this in a sketch. I was coming down 6th aveLnue from where I had not been having lunch from where I had lunch already, it was during my lunch-hour-or-so. There was the customary crowd of scattered persons, and of course I was just through watching two workboys play football against each other one on of the laughably original machines they have that there in the . . . nickelodeon-Automat→Penny Arcade (!) so and I stopped to watch to see and I am always curious, therefore. A woman this time (and that was one oddity!) was selling a humorous mechanical toy and I thought a fine thing for my son who will be born any month now and I felt warm inside; but the woman she was not very humorous it being cold outside and she looked around as though cops. The woman was ordinarily clean and nice and fat and eyes, she had on a coat trimmed with the ordinary fur, and she said no word which itself is bad tactics for one who wished to sell goods to a little crowd of people on the street. I thought I would buy it if it were not too cheap, but this is how it was: (I thought I would buy it on the spot)—it was a tiny mech. automobile with a coon driver that upended like a balking finicky horse providing the bystanders with much fun who were just wasting their time here in apathetic watchful waitfulness as it seemed. These crowds have no heart no soul no character no intelligence and their interest is an ugly thing. So I slightly thought but I was regarding the toy and the woman who was trying to sell them on the streets looking around every now to see if cops, and I knew this was a bad and cold season of the year many falling by the way, but those who had money and businesses sitting pretty, though tight. My own job was a sonofabitch thing, but I was anxious to forget that during lunchhours which come only once a day anyway. The woman was a pitiful creature rewinding the toy over and over, get a mechanical toy here, she said mechanically, perfunctorily lifeless, as she always set it down on the ground again to perform its tireless antics which became less and less funny and the people around became less and less interested, with no idea of buying. I don't know why I stayed; my time I knew would be soon up . . . but I was undecided, I had my eye on that little cute toy for maybe my son or (x) daughter though really that was a long time off; the different parts of the crowd leaving for various other removed places, and soon and all at once I was the only one remaining, the listless woman rewinding and about tired of talking the same words in the air which was cold and still looking foolishly around. Me, I was in a quandary or afraid to ask the price if she might say too much . . . I wondered why she did not announce the price, it was very poor street-saleswomanship, and I waited for her perhaps to say so. But she looked hopeless, probably she had no idea anyone would be silly enough to buy one and I wanted to badly, but it grew embarrassing and late and I shamefacedly whistled and sauntered slouched off away. But it annoyed me, it bothered me: I ask you, why should I have been undecided, and maybe I lost a chance right then and there to get a bargain and earn a *mitzvah*,[1] 2 things every good jew like myself wants to happen at the same time, and as they say in the bible I was sore troubled and that woman's pleading face was easy to remember. And I damned myself and hurried on there were few people walking the street now. And to tell you the truth, I almost . . . . on the way to the place, so cold was the day. But that is irrelevant, I suppose.

Transition, June 1929

BOOK REVIEW

A BOOKMAN'S DAYBOOK, by Burton Rascoe. Horace Liveright. $2.50

Mr. Rascoe is a Gentleman, a Scholar, and a couple of Old Ladies. He gossips interminably *of a luncheon for Hilaire Belloc, how Mencken and Nathan Play, laughing in the Algonquin, Rascoe's passion for trap drumming* . . . Oy, is dis a Boook! At times he attempts to be the Bold, Bad Iconoclast, (its a fashionable pose): "I think (he thinks,) that the Saturday Evening Post is more authentically literary than the Atlantic Monthly." Oooh, girls, aint he rough! But for the most part he is charming, subtile, and occasionally quite witty. A worm in the belly of the worm in the belly of the bookworm . . .

New Masses, June 1929

[1]Heavenly reward for a good deed.

FOG

where mumbling monstrosities pass me in the fog,
along little streets seen criss-cross-wise,
I go . . .
(at night, the spice of silent places
in my throat, drinking in oblivion)
to some quite house, removed from sight of men,
where I shall learn the meaning of lascivious repose.
I grope my way; I go . . .

now I can glimpse its woodwhite porch,
dewdamp; the shutters closed.
the open little door . . .
(surely I've been there before!)
within, a fire burns in the stove.
the clock tick-tocks . . .
here one reads books
as in a separate world,
tiny, selfenclosed, complete.

outside, the dullrain, fog, a blowing hateful gale;
oh I would fold within myself,
remove into the recess of a slightlysmelling room.
sour meat boiling in a round black pot.
a darkeyed woman shall appear, invite . . .
a plausible retreat!
yet I am lost now, in the fog . . .

(and we shall frolic on a field
imaged in a joyous world,
tiny, selfenclosed, complete.
and I shall learn the meaning of lascivious repose.)

though I still tramp the paved vague streets,
each step a flat click on the walks . . .
and low roofs brood, and beckon.

the world is stone, but fog
fog, is a pleasant myth.

Contemporary Verse, July 1929

FLATBUSH AFTERNOON

daytime slumbers on a cool midwinter in flatbush.
nothing much even poets can care to say now.
don't make talk talk here; here no mysteries.
autocars ask no questions;
    storekeepers ask no questions;
        politely inviting customers . . .
ladies with dogs, with lap dogs
    with lap-lap dogs
        ladies pass serenely,
totally unconscious; total wrecks
    of women—spayed
    hens.
daytime in midwinter flatbush sunnily
    yawns—not cold,
    not warm; polite.
courteously expects no commotion
    in the clean quiet streets
    below, here a dull hell
for angry devils like me.
move south, west, east,
    young men.
try the bronx or canarsie,
    expect no mysteries
    in polite streets.

New Masses, August 1929

WEISS IS WRONG

(Editors' Note: The July 1929 "Letters from Readers" column of *New Masses* carried a letter from Henry George Weiss of Tucson under the heading "Give Us Poems for Workers." He wrote: "Comrades: I have a criticism to make. The prose of the *New Masses* seems far away and ahead—revolutionarily speaking—of its poetry. Such poems as *Oswald the Bald*, the ones written by Herman Spector and other vers librists, are extremely clever, display in lots of cases masterly technique of that form of expression; but it is—you must admit—highly sophisticated verse, in fact depending for its appeal on an understanding of such art-forms. Such understanding the average working stiff does not possess, nor, everything considered, can be expected to possess at this stage of the game." The next month Spector's letter to Mike Gold appeared in the same column. The next May a Weiss letter complained that Spector "is beset with the chase after form.")

Dear Mike:

July *New Masses* is great stuff. Joe Kalar, Chas. Harrison, Frederic Cover, Ed. Falkowski and Mike Gold on Floyd Dell give me solid pleasure.

However, I don't pretend to understand any of your more intricate art theories. I don't agree with Henry George Weiss and I don't think I have any mastery of forms or that I am especially sophisticated. The fact that he mixes me up with H. H. Lewis shows he is considering "vers libre" very casually —but what the hell.

I will never write until I can breathe more freely. I assure you there is no fun being a proletarian and listening to discussions of "revolutionary art" when it stands to reason you can't slave 12 hours a day like a slob and create any kind of art at the same time.

Best wishes,

Bronx, N.Y.   Herman Spector

New Masses, August 1929

LONE CAT

Capslanty slouching-wise,
melachrino-mannered gentry go
precisely figured on the walls and walks
through cold drugged nights.

in vacuum of busytown,
electric-signs are on and off:

PRINCE MATCHIABELLI SMOKES OUR CIGARETTES!

(. . . *Who the hell are YOU?*

a constant deferential question,
finally answered in the lone cat's howl:
howwlll, grating upon the sense.

through cold drugged nights
melachrino-mannered gentry go,
precisely figured on the walls and walks.)

a single sob emits a glowing lamp
where houses feel each other's side
frightened, cold.

Palo Verde, 1929 (published as "Spics By Evening")

YES, WE HAVE NO VALHALLA

a high tentative note,
the clarinet calls
a question . . . and the music stops.
it passes out of the blood.
it is gone.
into no tearful stillnesses
nor echoes of thought remain
it has gone . . .
honor the surging lusts,
honor the seas, in memory!
they have passed, out of the blood,
and we know them no more.
the marching tunes, and low
sad, jazz songs—
a clarinet calls a question
once, and the music stops . . .

honor our seas, in memory!
honor the fierce, lost lusts!

Palo Verde, 1929

TWO CITIES

Three months I had been out of work. It was winter, the days were clear and cold, people passed by wrapped in coats their faces ruddy breathing mist, the chestnuts roasted fragrantly on corners by the parks, and outside department-stores the tinkling bells, Salvation Army grafters pimping christ.

I hardly noticed anything of what passed about me, each day I had grown more and more lackadaisical, dull, despairing. My nerve had gone, I was will-less, I had lost all self-respect. My eyes looked out with abject horror at the world, at the prospect of a lonely, degraded death; I could not sleep in the park any more but shuffled through the streets at night, the chill blasts choking my sobs and roaring through my painful brain. Somewhere waited a wife, somewhere two anxious little children whimpered from cold and hunger. I placed a clammy hand to my throbbing forehead, and retched. I moaned, with a sound as though something were being torn out of me. I was dizzy, vomiting like a drunk . . .

The night was an awful emptiness. Lamps glowed grinning like idiots. Occasionally a cab came jouncing by. The streets were black glass over which stray figures glided, vanishing ignominiously from sight. I trembled within me, it was cold, it was very cold. Stumbling below huge buildings of commerce, listening to the wash of rain in the gutters, I could not feel I had any real existence, but thought I lay trapped in a horrible dream, and I stared at the distant streets with vague incredulity. It could not be a man, in a city of men, who suffered thus! No!—A dim underground murmur, the wash of the rain in gutters, trickled ceaselessly.

I walked on and on. Suddenly I was in the deepest part of the slums. Tenements stood dazed under the ether of night, gnawed by the rain and the frost, rotten with filth. The wind wheezed through the streets, and the slum sighed, and the signs swaying in the wind creaked. Here is no sleep, but brief pause between ominous labours, a fitful relapse into death . . . I groaned. We shall have no rest all our lives long, we shall know no peace. I passed familiar alleyways, dark deserted side-streets, the grim story of this place upon my lips and in my heart. I passed furtively, with fists clenched . . .

. . . shimmering, somewhere, high like a symbol, a sign, to my glazed hopeless eyes, a great electric message in the night sky. Alone, aimlessly moving in the dead city, I wondered as the thing began to gleam more definite; now white, now red, approaching. What beacon is this, I thought, what salve to the tortured, what promise of faith to the lowly, degraded . . . I remembered the pleasant gospels of Jesus . . . *TUDOR CITY* (It flashed into my sight)— T U D O R   C I T Y ! —

I burst into a mad laugh that echoed through vast caverns of houses in successive waves of awakening sound. The rich had built a city within the city! At the very outskirts of the slums black, melancholy, beside the busy slaughter-houses, rose tall glittering towers, wall-encompassed exquisite gardens, magnificent festive halls! The signs blazed ferociously: *Tudor City!* And precise certain limousines rolled in and out the guarded gates. The gospels of Jesus—they are fulfilled!—these are the meek who have inherited earth!—

Then let me be cunning, I whispered, and my words became a wind; a great strength filled me. Let me know that there are two worlds, two cities . . . Everywhere they are tinkling pious bells, it is the season now to point the eyes upward to heaven, and each day our lot becomes more and more difficult to bear, we grow wretched and our patience wears thin . . . a city for the rich, and a city for the poor! Good!—Hoohhhnck? With a musical interrogative toot, and backward blur of swift smoke, a towncar passed smoothly . . . And it seemed that the wind shrieked in sudden anger, vengefully it smote and whipped and lashed everywhere about—rising from the slums it gathered untold force and fury until I thought the gleaming towers trembled at their base . . .

The gray dawn was approaching. I knew I must have a job, and I cursed hysterically. A job? . . . I thought of those I had held. In the lumber yards, twelve hours a day, the evil grub and relentless toil; on the railroads, men with arms and legs lopped off, crippled and strained, fearful of momentary dismissal; in the factory, wages below existence-level, all the bloody slavery of a sweatshop; in the warehouses, on the wharves, in ships, on roads, in the belly of the earth or high above it . . . Keep your lousy jobs, shrewd sneering Bosses! Who needs your jobs? Me?—you Bastards! . . . The gray dawn had come already. I sat down in the park and slept. All about me roared the city, whirling in spasmodic flashes of life, but I did not care, I did not know. I dreamed of a city for the rich, and a city for the poor.

New Masses, December 1929

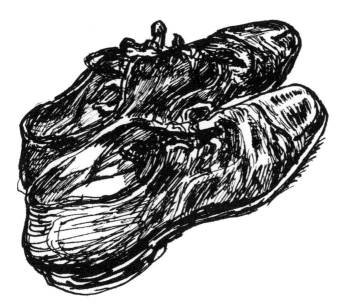

DOUBLE-MINUS ZERO

LAST NIGHTS OF PARIS, by Phillippe Soupalt, Macaulay Co. $2.50

I expected a good story from this French writer, who has been sentimentally described by blurbists as a member or ex-member of the dadaist and surrealist groups who nevertheless or necessarily therefore retains an enviable amount of individuality in technique and viewpoint. However that be, and I must admit that such descriptions usually fascinate me no end, I felt myself left at the end of this book without even the smell of a good story. And that is just a terrible shame, I think. Because when a writer sets out to draw a picture of Paris, and the Paris of the underworld at that, and *by night!*—well, I expect something for my money.

But the materials used are beyond the author's grasp. Crooks, pimps, exquisitely simple whores move in an atmosphere of cigarette-smoke and fog at dawn over impervious pavements, and there are isolated descriptions of noctural isolation that rival, somehow, similar things of Boris Pilnyak's; but as a novel, *Last Nights of Paris* just does not register. It is the old symbolist army game; nothing is created but symbols out of which minus nothing is created in turn. The result being double-minus zero.

New Masses, January 1930

CONFABS IN COFFEE POTS

Congenial coffeepot chauffeurs converse:
Decide vast issues in a cigarette-puff
    of smoke.
Conducive to conclusiveness,
      the fetid atmosphere

Swirls about the slanty caps
And the cocksure cups
Of coffee, hot:
      Half-and-half
Or black.

Late . . .
      an emptiness,
      a gray despair
      creeps into heart . . .
What lurks somewhere?
They turn; afraid, and peer;

Then backward turn, wisecracking
      of a dame or horse
      or a prizefight seen
In a similar atmosphere . . .

somewhere an emptiness,
the gnawing sense of waste.

Aw—sh—!
They spit, they smoke, they curse—
Congenial coffeepot chauffeurs,

CONVERSE.

New Masses, March 1930

THE GOLD NUGGETS

Joe Paladino worked in a warehouse near the Harlem River, lifting rolls of carpet to wherever he was told to lift them. Usually that was: Up. They were damn heavy rolls too, you would never guess how heavy until you tried lifting one yourself, and beside the carpet, there was the linoleum. It was the linoleum that did for Joe, in the end. He was never such a strong guy; he had been ruptured twice already, and would give a lot to get a softer job some place. But try and get it. Yeah.

Joe had been out of work before. So it was enough that this job seemed steady, and he was even able to buy a little furniture, and a radio, on the installment plan, and move in with the wife to a flat in the Bronx, a block away from the Third Avenue El, and a five-minute walk from Crotona Park.

The park! Every morning Joe took the kid there, listening to its gurgling delight, and watching it play with dirt. Joe taught it how to sift out the little stones in the hand, opening the fingers a little, and he shouted to the kid: Look—gold nuggets! And the kid shrieked joyously, and ran to carry little fistfuls of dirt to his hand. Ah, thought Joe, it's great to be a married man—to have a woman who cares for you and looks after you, and rubs your body with alcohol when you come home limp after a tough day, aching all over; and it's great to have a sweet little flower of a kid, to hold it up in the air and kiss its little behind, and every day to see it grow. Great stuff! Yeah.

Joe was what you might call a glutton for punishment. By his wan face and the distended veins in his arms you could see that he could not last long on the job, but must end by becoming miserably punch-drunk, and he would be of no use to anyone, not even himself. But a wage slave lives from one day to the next, and if tomorrow brings no worse than today, OK. Hold on to what you got, for the abyss yawns below. Joe was a young man, but his mind was old and tired. And his wife, too, though she looked so neat and dainty, she was no spring chicken now. At the age of eleven she had been scrubbing other people's floors for them, and then the factories got her, and kind of spoiled her complexion for good. She was very thankful to get married, and she loved Joe very much. It was hard to manage, but she managed. She didn't have it so bad off like the taxi-driver's wife who lived next door, whose husband left her for weeks at a time when work was slow, and came back soused. The taxi-driver's wife swore that some day he would not find her there when he came back, but so far he always had, and took it as a matter of course that she would be there, with all three kids cowering around her, and only a ludicrous show of defiance. So Joe's wife thought she was very lucky to have such a good husband. And Joe thought it was great to be a respectable citizen earning twenty-two dollars a week, and actually to have a little time in the evening to smoke and read a newspaper, and to be able to get a seat on the train, sometimes going home. They were very, very simple people.

Things got a little slack in the carpet line, though it seemed to Joe that the carpets were just as big and as heavy as usual. And they were beginning to notice that he was not the strongest man in the world. There was a big German Jew named Laber, who did unloading work downstairs at the track, and he had been laid off last week. He lived on Suffolk Street, downtown, had four young children, and always brought big baloney sandwiches for lunch. Laber used to tell Joe how he used to be a big candy-storeowner on the east side, but his oldest boy Hymie ruined his business by eating all the stock. Now that Laber was out, Joe was supposed to do his work too. Joe was energetic, quick, and knew the knack of lifting from long practice, so the foreman thought he would hold on to him and let Laber go. Laber had a dazed look when he got the bounce. What wage slave hasn't? The job is hell, it stinks, and the only thing worse is to lose the job. Who knows what happened to the beefy German Jew? Who cares? He was swallowed up, perhaps, in a murky sea of want-ads, begging, bosses' refusals, sneers, starvation, garbage-bits of tragedy, futile clutching-at-wisps. Joe forgot all about Laber. His big worry was how to keep the job.

The warehouse, at intervals, was supplied with Big Business Bulletins from the main offices of Fifth Avenue. These bulletins were countersigned by geniuses who had probably studied the Psychology of Leadership at school. They were intended to bulldoze little fellers like Joe Paladino. For example, they said: "Ideas? Have you any Ideas of how to do the job better, more efficiently? Let us know. Don't hide your light under a bushel." Joe tried to think of some good ideas, of how to do the job better. But he needn't have troubled. The geniuses worked it all out by themselves, in a cute, ingenious way. They laid off a goodly part of the force, and made the rest do double the work for the same money. Or rather, for less money, as they put in a new Golden Rule about working overtime for nothing. You don't have to go to college to think them things out. On the other hand, maybe you do. At least, you must keep far away from the lifting end of the game. Those that lift can never qualify as geniuses to Help Make Business Better. Joe Paladino would never have thought of clever Ideas like those on a bet. You have to hand it to the geniuses . . .

Grimly, Joe did what he was told to do. He was used to taking punches, and the Boss always hit below the belt. Mornings, he had to be dragged out of bed. He lived in a stupor. No more walks in the park with the kid. The kid never saw him, hardly. He came home nights, when the streets seemed to be melting from the heat under the glaring lamps, and his wife arose from sleep to put his food on the table and wash the dishes. And every day, the job became less secure. It was a question as to how much longer Joe was going to be allowed to remain a respectable citizen earning twenty-two dollars a week. A question that was pondered long upon, undoubtedly, by the geniuses. And the conclusion was: we can afford to let this man go. Scientific, impersonal—

just like that. A simple matter of mathematics. Profit and loss. On Saturday the foreman called Joe aside and sweetly told him he was fired. Why? Why? (Can you beat it, Joe had the nerve to ask why!) The foreman looked sorely at him. "When ya took dat last carload of linoleum down, I seen how ya got scared y'might hoit yaself, and you was too slow too. We can't have no weak guys workin here. Dat's all."

Returning home, there was a seething in Joe's brain. He looked out of the windows of the El at the fantasmagorical blur of buildings, passing a rapid succession of alternate 3 room flats, exactly like his own. All these people—poor slobs like himself—vainly trying to build a home and happiness on the treacherous sands of a job—bringing up kids whose future, wrapped in mist, was at the mercy of a rubicund cigarsmoking boss who operated at central offices and employed impersonal, scientific geniuses to contrive plans for efficiently running the plant—he felt like yelling into the tenements: Stop! Think! What do our lives hold for us? Are we worms? Are we men? Why should we take it on the button instead of hitting back? Stop! . . . It was another stifling night. He grunted to his neighbors, grouped around the stoop. They were all old before their time. There was the skinny, hysterical Jewess who was always screaming at her kids. She had been sent to the bughouse twice. There was the taxi-driver's wife. She had a goiter. The doctor told her to eat only soft foods, and try not to have another baby. There was the fruit-peddler; he had diabetes and varicose veins; his wife had cancer. Plenty of diseases to go around. The Boss hands them out unstintingly. Joe climbed up the stairs, stopping a while at each landing.

He pushed open the door, and was in the kitchen. He turned on the light. A few cockroaches hurried to shelter. Joe studied the oilcloth design on the floor. There was a stink of dead rat in the plaster walls. Well, they would have to get out of here. The furniture people would be on their heads in a week or two: a marshall would bust in the door and take all the stuff out. What if they had paid in over a hundred dollars on it? The law was made by businessmen for businessmen. Laborers exist only to make such people fat. It was all written down, a cultured terminology, on legal-looking documents.

She was still sleeping. Dog-tired. Recently she had been taking in homework from the factories, because they were going to have another kid, and that was an expense. Joe shook her a little, and she sat up swiftly. She saw by his face what it was all about. Clasping him in her arms, she sobbed noiselessly. The kid would have to go to a nursery again. Gee, that was tough. Now the kid lay in trusting sleep in the crib. And what about the next one? Joe's wife got up dully and put supper on the table. A man must eat. Gee, she was a good woman.

Haggard and worn they awoke in the morning. Sunday. It was very, very silent in the house. After breakfast, Joe picked up the kid and went to the park. The kid chattered in funny, original vocables. Picking a fairly clean

74

spot on the grass, Joe lay down in the sun and let the kid run around and play. His head ached like hell. He felt like vomiting. The kid came running up with a little fistful of dirt, shrieking joyously: Ooh! Gold nuggets! Gold nuggets! . . . Joe took the dirt in his hand, and sifted out the little stones. Gold nuggets. Yeah. So's your old man. Pah! His hand clenched them fiercely, and he flung them away. They're stones!, he hollered at the kid—Stones!

New Masses, September 1930

CONDUCTOR 1377

The traction company was advertising for men, thirty-five cents an hour, motormen and conductors. On account of my bad sight I picked a spot as conductor, because they wouldn't take a motorman who wore glasses. I got my slip OK'd, paid 1.65 for a badge, and was shipped up to the doctor's office. He passed me. I went back to the office, signed up to buy a uniform at the regulation comm. store, which happened to be Browning & King, well known clothiers for the elite; signed the other articles which said I was a member of the Brotherhood; then I went back to the parkbench. I had a job.

The next day I plunked down 22.50 for a swell new suit, and a nice braided cap, and reported back to the Instruction Department. Here they were going to teach me how to be a conductor, and they didn't charge me anything either. It was all free. This company didn't care damn about expense, so long as things were done right.

The instructor was a beefy, redheaded guy who acted like a real pal. He was very encouraging. The first thing he taught us was how to count, so we wouldn't never mix the company's money with our own. If we did, that was just too bad for us. He proved that in black and white. He showed us how the clock worked, and explained that if we would ever have any doubt about how many fares to ring up, we should always ring up a few extra, just to be on the safe side. All in all, he acted like a real pal.

Well, we all passed with AAA marks from this guy, or at least we all passed. We had our theories down pat, but were yet to put them into practice. The next grade was held in a real trolley-car down in the barns, under the tuition of a comical old boy who reminded me of Emil Jannings playing the After part in those Before and After dramas. This guy didn't like me. I laughed at his jokes, but I laughed too long, not giving him hardly enough time to get off another one. Finally he glowered over at me until I thought maybe he wouldn't pass me, and me with 22.50 plus 1.65 in the pot, so I shut up for a while. He was really such a comical guy, with a walrus moustache, bullet head, built like a mack truck especially the bulldog waddle he had. He was an honorary member of every cops and detectives organization in the city. He thought all jews were lawyers.

When we had got OK'd by this punk, we were still goofs, you understand. We had to work-out for a week or so at the company's own expense, no extra charge, alongside the horny-handed veterans. They usually picked guys with a few stripes for this duty, trusted members of the Brotherhood, and paid them fifty cents extra a day—big money. The guy I was working with the first day had a bad habit of trying to push me out of the car when I didn't lean out far enough to please him. I had to call him down for it, and that got him disgusted with me, so he did all the work himself, and wouldn't even talk to me. I wasn't sore. In fact, I was sociable. I offered to collect the nickels while he looked after the passengers getting on and off, but I could see he didn't trust me. Well, he signed my card as OK for the day, and I felt a little happier.

The next day I thought sure I was capable to be a conductor. I knew about counting scores, waiting for the green light, seeing that no passengers were unavoidably killed, and how to be polite though firm. "Step right up in the car!", I shouted. It was a grand job, even if I hadn't collected a cent on it yet.

Around about the third day I was doing things for myself, I had sort of got the rift, but wasn't getting paid for it. It was disgusting. Here I was getting up out of the hay at four-thirty a. m., out on the rails at five-fifteen, sweating myself silly for at least ten hours, counting up the boss' money at the end of the day on my own time, and nary a one of them nickels found its way to my pocket. It was fierce, and some of the guys had to give it up, and tried to sell their uniforms second-hand to new men or such, but found mighty few buyers.

When about a week had passed in this wise, more or less, and I was about thinking maybe I ought to apply for a job as instructor, they put me on the payroll, with many buts and howevers. That is, I was an extra man, I had to hang around the barns from godknowswhen in the morning to whocares at night, and maybe, if somebody got sick or something terrible happened, they would call me for two or three hours work, perhaps, thirty-five cents an hour. So I did that little thing for them. During the time we were waiting to be called we were told to cling close to the company restaurant run exclusively by the Brotherhood, of which we were all members. Here we were allowed to buy soggy doughnuts and drink some kind of stuff out of chipped cups which stunk like rats. I didn't think I could stomach that kind of stuff, but you'd be surprised what waiting around in a carbarn all day long will do to a guy. I even ordered meat-dishes in that dive, and now I can understand what happened to the old trusty nags when they scrapped the horsecars. But the carbarns were a great educational center.

New Masses, December 1930

UNEMPLOYED

After a morning of pounding the pavements in search of a job, answering Want-Ads for any kind of dirty, ill-paid work available, a guy feels that he's just about done-up, and is entitled to a rest. There's no point in plugging at it any longer: after eleven o'clock there's nothing doing. Some guys go straight from the joblines to the breadlines. But I had a few pennies left. So I headed for an automat, thinking to warm up with what I call a "coffee-minus", before spreading myself around in my various hang-outs: the 42nd Street Library, free art galleries, penny arcades, etc.

It was too damn cold to walk around much. The wind was hitting it up with a vengeance; a thin, cruel glaze of sleet covered the streets. Pushing through a revolving door, I found myself in the warm, clean-looking restaurant: milkwhite tables glistening all around, people furtively or thoughtfully munching their food, the glint of nickel and neat, clever dishes spotlighted behind glassware like star performers in some vaudeville show. There's nothing that appeals more to the ordinary New Yorker, in weather like this, than an unpretentious, busy cafeteria. In the first place, it has a sort of tabloid look: bright, easy to understand, and optimistic. In the second place, it clicks, and that makes it authentic.

So I held the knob just a little longer than was necessary, and the last drop of coffee dribbled into my cup, and the guy behind me was ready to curse with impatience. Choosing a vacant table, I sat down and slapped my paper down beside me. Other people, I noticed, were sitting alone by preference, and silently regarded each other. Cynical lot of egotists, I thought. I sipped the coffee: it was delicious.

Through the plate-glass window I could see Sixth avenue, the pillars of the El, the cheerless plot of park beyond: bare now, rimmed with ice and snow. The good warm coffee inclined me to take a better view of life. Things are bound to change, eh? A guy can't go on existing like this forever. How long, now, have I been on the bum? Oh, pretty long, a pretty long time. Being battered around gets a fellow dizzy: his memory goes back on him. Or maybe—there is too much to remember. Well it does not matter: nothing matters, much. I drank the coffee slowly, not to lose any of the flavour.

The last night had been a tough one. I'd caught a little sleep on the trains. At 14th an accident had tied up the line for over an hour. A guy had knelt down on the platform as the train pulled in, and flung himself over. A sudden shower of sparks, the engineer's quick fearsome *Toot!* as the train grinded to a full stop in the center of the platform, and it was all over—for him. It was messy. Parts of him were found as far back as the third car. The pavement below had received a fresh, steaming gift of his intestines. In the morning paper I noticed the item:: "GROUND TO DEATH UNDER 'L' TRAIN— Body Mangled Beyond Possible Identification." I watched while the emer-

gency crew collected all the pieces—large pieces and when they called out, "All Aboard!", went back to the car again and carelessly stretched out to sleep. But as the train rumbled and clattered heavily, ponderously on, while the still night grew colder and colder, and crystallized into dawn, I dreamed . . . of huge steel wheels rolling and rolling, wet with blood, with snowflakes that melted instantly upon contact with the metal; of huge steel wheels grinding and spattering bones and flesh; of upraised arms, mute mutilated torsos, guts. . . .

Gar: will I be next, then? They had found his hat lightly poised between two ties, untouched. The engineer was a tall, fat, smiling chap, wearing a cap too small for his head. This was the tenth he'd "got," he said. The other nine hadn't been so lucky: they'd lived—for awhile. Like a thunderbolt in my brain, the question: What thoughts had this human being entertained, while he deliberately kneeled and measured the distance from himself to the monster train, approaching? Was he any more miserable than I? Why was I so anxious to keep my own guts inside me?—

I took my eyes away from the grim pillars of the El. Forget it: it won't do you any good. I reached for my paper. It was no longer on the seat beside me. I looked up. A heavy-set fellow had seated himself at the table, and was reading it.

I guess I was past feeling uncommonly jumpy. Anyhow, I had a bad shock. The guy sitting there so calmly, reading the day's news, was the suicide of the night before! This impression was so strong and startling, that for the moment, I could not move. Integrated again were the large pieces and the small pieces: the shoulder with gaping wound where the head had been, pinned beneath the carriage of the train, the bits of flesh and bone strewn along the rails, the mangled legs, the hat jauntly reposing upon the crossties, the blotch of guts in the center of the gleaming crosstown trolley-tracks about which an awed crowd had collected; the body was made whole again, animated with moods and visions, it was turned into a jobseeker again, words spelled out backwards, a movie wound up wrong. With a wrenching effort of the will, I closed my eyes . . . and the obsession passed. I felt my cheeks wet with tears, and inwardly cursed my weakness. Gulping the last of the coffee down, I glared squarely at the man.

He looked like a truckdriver or dishwasher, with a strong skull and serious, squinted eyes. Laboriously he pored over the Want-Ads, much pencilled by my own hand, and evidently found little that was encouraging. Somehow this big fellow seemed pathetic to me. He had muscles to heave a case or lift a great log, yet these muscles were valueless to him. Civilization had outsmarted men like him; machines had made a mockery of their strength. He glanced up from the paper and looked at me dully. He was intimidated by all the bustle and activity of a big city, which now bore no relation to his needs. I could read fear in his eyes. Probably the man had a family. Would he starve then? Would he turn bandit, or beg? I saw him look out the plate-glass window, at the base, relentless streets, and I saw a shudder pass over him.

I would have spoken to him, I think, and he would have responded in puzzled, sullen monosyllables, evasively, but an ejaculated greeting startled him, and he turned around. A little, weazened youth shook his hand and sat down beside him. It was lunch-hour; the place was crowding up with hurried diners.

The newcomer was comical with his air of animation and self-assurance. Well Jim, whatcher doin'? What's new—nothin'? Still lookin' around fer somethin', eh? 'Stough. More 'n more guys outa woik, they say, than ever before. But wot's de use o' hangin' crepe, I say to 'em. I just got a raise, coupla months ago. I ain't got nothin' to kick about. Know dat dame I useter go out wid?—Jim nodded—Well, I got anudder now. Boy, you wanner see her: Some dame. Nifty. See dis suit?—Jim saw it—Dis ain't no 22.50 rag. Feel it: go ahead, don't be afraid. Some cloth, eh? All wool and a yard wide. Forty-two bucks is wot dis stood me.

The little fellow sort of squared off, pugilistically, daring the other to disbelieve him. Then he went on: Ya got be pretty smart, nowadays. I don't let nobody put nothin' over on me.

He was full of small talk. Finally, he got up. Aincher gettin' nothin', Jim? Coffee? No?—He hesitated for a moment. —Well, I guess I'll get me some ham 'n eggs . . . And he walked off toward the counter, a little wiseguy in natty clothes, cocky, puny, and puerile. The man called Jim kept gazing soberly out at the streets, the lines around his mouth deepened, despair in his eyes, unconscious defeatism in slouched shoulders and apathetic hands.

Sure you'll get a job soon, Jim. You gotta live, eh? You gotta be smart, that's wot. Jumping under a train won't help very much. Naw. On the other hand, maybe you were not cut out to be a little pimp. Nature fashioned you differently. It's a problem, Jim, it's a "problem."

So I got up, feeling a little empty and jagged and not so steady on my pins, and shuffled over to the 42nd Street Library, to read a book.

When I got down near the Library, I got thinking about Jim. Funny the ideas a guy gets on an empty stomach. But I thought I'd hate like hell to be in Jim's way if he and a lot of others got it into their heads to go out and *take* enough to eat, job or no job. I'd been hearing some of them talk that way.

New Masses, February 1931

WORKERS' ART

A monthly department for reports and discussion of Workers' Cultural Activities.

Credo of a Soviet Movie Director

1. The essential difference between the Soviet cinema and all other cinema is the absence, in our production, of commercial goals. The Soviet cinema is an educational and artistic institution.

2. This situation places the director in an exceptionally favorable position. The Soviet director can devote more time to questions of form, to experimentation and to a profound examination of the content of this film.

3. I am an Ukranian director.

4. I have produced three important films: *Zveni-Gora, Arsenal, Soil.* In the first I endeavored to show the status of an Ukranian village in 1929, that is, at a time when there were taking place transformations not only of an economic nature, but also changes in the mentality of the masses.

5. For these three films I assembled a social documentation. I showed our land; its history, customs, social conditions, its struggles and ideals.

6. My principles are:

(a) I have no interest in stories in themselves. I use them only to the extent that they are useful in giving a maximum translation of important social forms;

(b) That is why I work upon typical documents and apply the synthetic method. My heroes are representatives of their class. Their actions likewise.

(c) The documentation of my films is con-centrated at times to the very limit; at the same time I pass it through the emotional prism. I never remain indifferent before documents; one must know how to love fully and strongly, and also to hate, otherwise, all works remain dogmatic and dry.

7. I utilize actors, but more so people chosen from crowds. My documentation requires this. One must not fear people who are not professional actors. One must well remember that every man can act perfectly for the screen at least once.

8. When I choose professional actors, I make every effort to see to it that their roles in the film do not impress the spectator with their profession.

9. Out of the consideration to the other persons in my films, I use every method which will permit me to obtain desired results with the least possible difficulty.

10. I think that *Soil* will be my last silent film.

11. My next film will be sonal and talking and I hope that the application of words and sound will not make me deviate from the direction in which I have been working until now.

ALEXANDER DOVZHENKO
(*Translated from the French by S. Brody.*)

Chicago Exhibit

The Palm Club of proletarian artists and writers will hold an art exhibition and dance on February 27 at the People's Auditorium, 2457 West Chicago Avenue, Chicago. The exhibit, arranged by Comrade Jan Wittenber, will consist of drawings and paintings by *New Masses* artists and members of the John Reed Club of New York, along with the work of a number of Chicago painters of note. A new collection of posters from Soviet Russia will be included.

The exhibit will also be on view at the Workers Book Store, 2021 West Division Street, Chicago, under the direction of S. H. Hammersmark.

Maurice Becker—New York painter, was one of the founders of the *Masses* in 1910.

Melvin P. Levy—critic, novelist, contributing editor to *New Masses* has just completed his third novel for early publication.

Jessica Smith—is author of *Women in Soviet Russia.*

Charles Yale Harrison—is author of *Generals Die in Bed*, published last year, and a new novel, *A Child Is Born*, now on the press.

Norman Macleod—editor of *The New Morada*, is also American editor of *Front*, published in Holland.

Herb Kruckman—young artist of White Plains, N. Y., makes his first appearance in *New Masses.*

William Siegel—New York artist, illustrator, is contributing editor of *New Masses.*

Herman Spector—Born 1905 in New York City, and has never been farther west than 10th Avenue. Left high school after three years, the loser in a passionate struggle for a vital education, to fulfill the prediction of a pedagogue: "You'll turn out to be a ditchdigger or a Bolshevik". Worked, toward this end, as lumber handler, shipping clerk, truck driver, streetcar conductor, laborer, baker's helper, W. U. "mutt", factory hand, butcher boy, envelope addresser, canvasser, soda jerker. Now married, father of a 3-year old girl, and engaged in writing a novel. Contributed to *Exile, The American Caravan, Free Verse, Anthology of Revolutionary Poetry, Transition, Unrest*, etc. Contributing Editor of *New Masses*. Member of the John Reed Club.

IN THIS ISSUE

Hugo Gellert—is now at work on a book of about 100 lithographs and text based on *Capital* by Karl Marx.

Langston Hughes—author of *Not Without Laughter*, published last fall, is now at work on a new novel. He has just been announced the winner of the Harmon Award for the most significant contribution in literature made by a Negro in the past year.

Jacob Burck—is staff artist on the *Daily Worker.*

Phil Bard—young New York artist, is a frequent contributor to *New Masses.*

Robert Cruden—Detroit auto worker, lost his job at the Ford factory in the recent general layoff.

I. Klein—contributor to the magazines, is executive board member of *New Masses.*

Agnes Smedley—author of *Daughter of Earth*, is now in Shanghai, China.

Otto Soglow—illustrator, cartoonist, is a frequent contributor to the magazines.

William Gropper—author of *Alay Oop!*, a story in pictures, has just returned from Soviet Russia.

Louis Lozowick—New York artist, is secretary of the John Reed Club.

announcing the first two numbers of

FRONT

a radical magazine in 3 languages and 3 editorial sections: USSR, Europe, USA.

FORD	BEHEIM-SCHWARZBACH
REGER	PLATOSCHKIN
BOYLE	MUENSTERER
INBER	VERESSAIEV
HARDY	YISHNEVSKY
JOHNS	TRETIAKOW
POUND	SALEMSON
BARBER	WILLIAMS
LAMOUR	SAVIOTTI
VITRAC	BOUSQUET
BOWLES	MACLEOD
BURZIO	McALMON
OUTKINE	HERBEIT
MACLEOD	CAYATTE
DALLEAS	ISRAEL
CAYATTE	MANGAN
ZUKOFSKY	PUTNAM
EINSTEIN	SCHEER
CALVERTON	ALMON
LUGOWSKI	FITTS
RATHGEBER	JOLAS
REINHARDT	POUND
TRETIAKOW	FORD
MUENSTERER	JIGA
VON WESTPHALEN	DUFF

american editor NORMAN MACLEOD
112 E. 19th St., Room 806, New York City
published from
15 Rietzangerlaan THE HAGUE Holland

CASH OR CREDIT

On Third Avenue the huge signs play
to make our city smile, be gay,
and BUY (the balmy saps,) TODAY.

Don't hesitate!
tomorrow it may be
Too Late!
the stores ope up their maws,
and wait.

it's winter, though these signs gleam warm.
crowds fill the sidewalks, gape, and swarm,
drift like the drifting snow upon a windowpane
in flakes that melt, and trickle down again.

they come, and watch the twitching of her thighs,
who writhes in orgiastic agonies:
a Poster-Whore, a slogan set in neon light,
green, purple, pink, far down the night
she imitates the sincere, fecund rut:

economy.
a pretty business in the great city.

    the world's a loop-the-loop,
    so ride!
    a gushing girl,
    a lovenest bride!
    a train that shrieks on speeding thru the dark
    with insane joy (no pain)—a mark
    for your shrewd aim to hit, and win!
    a pocket where the ball rolls in!

    play ball! lets dance!—come;
    bottoms UP,
    we'll waste the inside of the cup!

    pay when you please,
    what matters it?
    we're here to serve,
    don't mention it . . .

Bedizened harlot, how you loathe
the ugly slums that you have made,
and fester in!
the words men use to tell your trade,
the consequences of your sin,
are lost in the ostentatious din
and clatter of your jaws:

BUY NOW,
we furnish happy homes . . . 5 dollars down
and a year to pay,
your money goes a long, long way . . .
with us.

Advertising's a shameless jade,
wise in the tricks
of the trade,
cunning and vicious;
glib with the glibness of thieves,
formal and legal and specious . . .
palming off paste as the "real ice",
selling gold bricks at a "big sacrifice":

    just five dollars down,
    and a Year to pay . . .

(and just five dollars missing
a month or a week,
and you can be kissing
what you've PAID, on the cheek . . .)

On Third Avenue the huge signs play
to make our city smile, be gay,
and BUY (the balmy saps,) TODAY.

New Masses, March 1931

BUM'S RUSH

Time passed, the corner was bowery and houston, saturday becoming sunday but slowly, vaguely, indistinct. They were tearing up roads there somewhere, lights blinked from the pit, scraps and strips of tin and things littered alongside. Time, in a fragmentary casual manner passed, surprised at itself, in spurts, in spasms. Suddenly there was a rush of figures, and suddenly there was not, and stillness. What was it all about? Was all this talk of unemployment and what do you think might happen next the rot, was it true—what? Pavolovsky clutched at the supports at the bottom of the stairway to the El, saying goodbye to his young friend Alex, trying to be heard above the rasp and roar of a train, something important, something to show he was nobody's fool, on the tip of his tongue. Pah! What was the good of it all, anyway? Alex perhaps politely believed that he was nobody's fool but it was not evident, no he could see that, it was not evident. The train rattled in passing, moaned, died away: he ahd and awd. No, he must find the word. Everything was up in the air yet. Off the earth.

Pavolovsky was a queer creature, one of those bohemians always explaining himself away, always getting drunk with self-love, with beautiful dreams of creation, planning in an hour novels, allegories, essays, epics, tales, tragedies, burlesques, in marvellous detail and with true Villonesque aplomb, but it was all conversation, nothing ever came of it. Whereas Alex was silent and serious; he listened to everyone, never saying an unnecessary word: it was whispered he was doing a book. Now he was listening to Pavolovsky, he would say nothing disparaging to Pavolovsky, he would not think of doing so, and that is why Pavolovsky despaired, and groped for the word, gesticulating frantically: it took all the wind out of his sails. TIME WAS PASSING. Where had the word gone? Another train came, with breakers of sound rushing over Pavolovsky: he gasped and spat. When it was gone he looked after it with redrimmed resentful eyes, and was about to speak. Pah, what was the use of it all anyway?

A bum, in the passing of a moment, turning 'round and walking slant-wise as a spinning top, gyrated and hesitated, blubbered something from blabbing lips to Alex and the bohemian by the steps to the El, what did he say, they leaned forward, but it was nothing, just a panhandler, muttering. An auto whirled and bounced past the corner, within plainly visible a party of wallstreet clerks in sailorsuits and tamashanta-girls on laps blowing tin-horns, some celebration, confetti, blah. I am always drunk blubbered the bum, he had a head like a peanut, wore a comical cap on it, smiled flushed foolish maundering like a child, gyrated and turned, turned slantwise, surprised at himself, at his motions, changing place with rapidity and indirectness. Always drunk—every day every week—his weak chin saggily sunken. He reversed himself on staggering limbs like a toy that had been wound up and would not stop, blabbing in the midst of a group of tough gazabos, minute racketeers, glorified gorillas standing waiting for someone to push over, some little guy: Gowan, they growled, grunted, scowled; made pushing gestures like they would smack him one maybe, hard: he gestured in return, cursed gowan, leered, feebly . . . circumvented paved squares and was peculiarly off in a sudden zigzag of determination. Pavolovsky whetted his thin lips: the word must come. It was time.

He looked down the desolate street, the bum was disappearing, there was a curious chromatism of patchwork sky and cigarette-signs, traffic symbols, coney island lurid tenements in purple, pink, rose-red. Ah what is life mused Pavolovsky for want of better musing. Under the El the trains pass and repass, and when they are overhead they drown out speech, and when they are gone they are gone, distressingly, and they have taken with them words—conversation,—scraps and strips and slats and planks of it, broken and floating; lunging, upjutting, sinking. Alex waited. My poor pale friend, thought Pavolovsky with compassion. Then the thought unpleasantly smote him that he was like an impotent person in the vacant presence of a lewd lovely gracious lady; and the word eluded him: his bewilderment exuded drops of sweat. And he thought: a man like me, what am I doing here? I am wasting my time. Why talk? Why?—but he persisted. It was necessary to explain. Again a bum came, groggy but sober, he wanted a light: Pavolovsky struck the match for him. The bum looked up out of bloodshot eyes—Tanks; tanks mistuh. . . . (strained, trembly,) Maybe in a day—maybe in a year. . . . And he swept around the corner, right boldly by the wise gazabos who were going different ways for the night, making wisecracks of goodbye to sustain themselves until the morrow, when they would awake with unvarying wisecracks of goodmorning, to sustain themselves for the day. The squarecut greenish overcoat of the bum, his soberfaced significance, bloodshot tragic eyes, stayed with Pavolovsky while time made three soldierly steps backward, wiggled, pirouetted, and burst into a machine-gun laugh.

The street was suddenly sloppy with ragged vagrants and bums; foolish, blowsy, leering, monstrous, staggering, crummy. The speakeasies had let out, other places had closed for the night, they were vomited from hallway to hallway. In a dirty gutter stream they would go down into the sewers with a gurgling noise, together with the dead already, the decaying and feces, with a stub of cigarette the stink of garbage and booze and some slight workings of a brain, eh what? Alex didn't see them, he had problems, he would do that book; the bohemian remembered a fine phrase from somewhere and it all came back to him, he hunched over his shoulders and exclaimed:

See!—everything that has happened to me, Alex, was necessary—that I may be what I am, that I may become what I wish to become—I know not what. So therefore everything is vital, so I embrace everything, and I am glad that what has happened has happened—you understand? But here Alex demurred, or seemed to demur, it was late, it was two o'clock, the clock in the Coffeepot in whose glare they now stood showed the white space of a circle that was somehow solemn and didactic; its two grim lines of hands cut it like a pie. One could eat pie now, Pavolovsky mused in his belly. A guy in an apron wheeled the big rusty stinking garbage can out onto the street, overflowing with slops, and dumped it with a clank and metallic thud on the walk. Slumgullion. They kept right on eating there in the Coffeepot, chauffeurs and loafers poking away crullers and stowing steaming coffee inside, where it made warmth, and the brain balanced and lightened and began to tick again, the joints loosened, fear and uncertainty vanished, what the hell, cigarettes after and saunter along chewing a toothpick, the world is under one's belt. Yes, Pavolovsky knew well the value of coffee. It made him what he was because he was, and that's good enough; and it caused the tongue to wag, which was pleasant, and a man could be gay and yet sad, boastful yet modest, sprightly without being womanish. Coffee, he ejaculated, is the american substitute for a soul!

Alex was thinking: I have met brilliant nuts on sparsely populated streetcorners at night, and they have referred me in a pinch to the science of Numerology and the philosophy of the "As-If", thinking thereby to increase an effect of sapience visible to all beholders. And I have met the blundering blusterers, trip-hammer economists, the world is so and so, thus and thus, you are what you are because you inevitably are. And I have listened, listened well, and I am convinced. In this life which has a past and a future, everything is part of something else, the machine is all, and nuts have their uses too. What they say is not important. Look well at their hands, their lips, their eyes; listen intently and you will detect in their voices the essential hysteria, braggadicio, fear: hah, now I have it. Pavolovsky has discovered that he is minus testes. He fondles ideas which he cannot master, he admires them with honest tears in his eyes, they appear the more sensuously beautiful as they are the more inaccessible. —Alex began slowly to smile a broad smile. . . .

Two bums coming by fouled each other out of sheer clumsiness and because they were mainly concentrated on each other, they fumbled and swore, and reeled apart. Overhead the trains rolled in and out, fewer now, more portentous rolling and rumbling, and the silence that was left was like a knife-thrust. On the corner the candystand man was putting up the boards, locking up, folding away his business-apron and preparing to waddle home in the respectable disguise of a private-citizen. His wife, who possessed immense buttocks, slept on her left side; and the odor that came from her mouth was exactly as the more cultured advertising writers have described. Alex felt it was futile to hang around this way. Politely, he decided, he would venture an abrupt query and Pavolovsky would be forced to dismiss himself. In the older man, however, there was some painful and abortive process taking place. It was as though hot coffee flowed in his veins. . . .

Out of the tightstretched darkness of the far street limped and shuffled a careless stooped beadyeyed bum, pausing a moment in the full sidewalk glare of the Coffeepot—FRANKFURTERS & BEANS 35—reached deep with claws of hands into the stinking garbage mess and plucked—HAM OMELETTE 40—some horrible tidbit; then turning and pawing it over and over, vacuous-lipped, passed with a loony bulging stare the two men in tortuous deliberations by the El, and returned, gleefully, into the dark, a rat with its prize: globbing it, gloating, crunching and wolfing it. . . .

Time, fragmentary, casual, passed,—the corner was bowery and houston, saturday becoming sunday but slowly, vaguely, indistinct. The word—where had it gone, the cocotte, the slut? Only static-dazed pavements veering and droning away in the distance . . . a train's roaring and moaning and dying. "It is an old, old world, my friend."

Pavolovsky spoke: A dime, Alex, er—carfare? —And Alex tendered it, and departed.

Front, April 1931

THOSE UNGRATEFUL MASSES

You give them a job; 16 hours a day.
Small coins that clink in their ragged pants;
You talk to them, too, in a fatherly way,
Tell them about that chance to advance—

And do they act peaceable, decent-like?
No—they shake their fists and go out on strike!

You tell them production has reached such a pitch
That every laboring sonofabith
Must pay for his labor by starving to death—
You tell them dying's good for the breath,

And do they succumb by gradual stages?
No—they meet and holler for WORK OR WAGES!

In the summer of course they drop like fleas,
In the winter they stiffen, and moan, and freeze;
The t.b. gets them and every disease
We've discovered for them in our efforts to please—

And do they welcome this clever solution?
NO—THEY ORGANIZE FOR REVOLUTION!

New Masses, September 1931

2ND AVENUE SWEAT

the train rears high over all this muck
of rusted iron and garbage dumps,
flowers and garlic, and windows choked
with faces bereft of color or hope . . .

the traffic roars, and stutters and drones;
the swish-puff of a power pump,
and sewer stinks; the unctuous voice
of a radio preacher: O come unto Jesus,
for he will save!
oliveoil, fruits, and the mouldy cheese
in markets where milling thousands sweat;
kids chatter like perky parakeets
as they dart around pushcarts and murderous wheels . . .

O come unto Jesus!
the brass-knuckled sun beats on our heads—
oh anywhere, anywhere out of the slums . . .
(for he will save,)

    on exclusive beaches,
    where preachers and pimps
    and their delicately nurtured mistresses
    gaze on a wide expanse of sea
    (it's a small world, after all)
    the gracious sun beams on the sands
    like the gentle jesus,
    like jesus indeed

    (for he will save,)
    and they lisp of love,
    of mysticism jesus and tea
    (with lemon in it)
    and they swim
    in serene blue waters . . .

but 2nd avenue is seething in sweat,
infants wail in close cribs of disease,
and girls like petulant blossoms wilt
in the hot, rank factories.

the train rears high over all this muck:
    (a small word explodes from a truckdriver's lips)
but on exclusive beaches they lisp:
it's a small world after all.

    O come unto Jesus!
    its 20% cooler.

New Masses, October 1931

TIMECLOCK

a big mack rolling and rumbling down the long street,
and lo, morning!
pavements glisten with cold assurance of concrete
achievement; cash-confidence exudes from roughspores of stone
(bigtime belching out of black funnels,)
and milliondollar plants white, virginal in the sudden sun,
tiers of windows rising sightless from moist sorrows of night;
radios fermenting blood with jazz.

john hawley awakes, an old weariness in young bones.
minutes are decisive units of salary,
looming largely upon the hideous timeclock,
ticking regularly.
he looks out the window, past the twisting el . . .
the scene is always the same:

each morning john hawley adorns his meekness
with a necktie flamboyant as a hollywood movie,
and emerges, whistling blithely, from a musty hallway,
the iridescent answer to a maiden's prayer.

each morning john hawley jaunts to the job
via streetcar in the summertime,
absentmindedly proffers his fare
(the motorman has a sweaty face),
turns to the sportsection of the paper with habitual indifference.

morning sizzles like something toothsome in vats,
preparing miraculous fodder for the keen appetite,
and the refreshed mind sniffs . . .

but he tracks timidly in unctuous labyrinths,
uprooted, clamped to revolving mechanisms
until evening comes
                                        an incubus,
stale with the stink of sweat, forgetful,
cold.

(a white collar clerk: an amorphous slug,
found in abundance in mire,

in fecund, obfuscate cities . . . disgusting to the touch.
thus the political dictionaries.)

laborers have souls that writhe
to the clattering crescendo of power-machines,
and little hunchbacked men dream and moan
where the wheels spin in rhythms upon the brain
like surf beating on the sloped shores,
but john hawley, a fileclerk, a catholic christian,
number 178, punching IN and OUT,
a pale young man wearing a kleenkut suit
and a straw hat in the summer
has been perforated, stamped:
AMERICAN MADE.
drugged by the clock portentously measuring
stingy minutes of salary,
the mind deformed and poisoned by headlines
("a paper for people who think")
to become the cruel convenience of capitalists:
the slave echoing the masters wish.

but at evening
john hawley, dropped like a plummet
past thirty-odd floors
reaches the street, and (somewhat dizzy),
feels the blood flowing back into veins
sapped by gestures of obeisance and meaningless
frivols of toil,
and bulbs enunciate time's wealth
out of confusion and weariness.

now the city froths insane at night;
its panting, throbbing breath
fogs the solitary lamps;
a restless humming underneath,
music of its peculiar fever . . .

john hawley is an entity
stifled by bricks and steel and electric-
lights,
wandering aimless, alone, through the ghoulish
squares.

freedom is a girl with tangled hair
whose breasts are worthy of caresses,
whose eyes, imperious with a larger lust,
vitriol the tissues of the virtuous;

out of the night, impassive, saying there is no god,
no caesar,
no allembracing goodness;
nothing, nothing, only stone . . .
she is a pretty piece
throwing kisses from a necessary distance,
singing throaty, sentimental songs
in a jazzband voice.

john hawley glimpsed,
through movies of incessant reels
(all-talking-dancing-whoring),
the dwindled whiteness of her thighs—
a super-super-nymph,

and walked
far
seeking her bed

the sky was endless, glimmering
into dawn . . .

and he crept, vanquished, an old weariness overcoming his bones,
past the garish sconce in the musty hallway,
painfully up the carpeted flights
to his room.

on the twisting el
trains scudded and droned;
he slept, respiring with the wind,
haggard as the gray, pitiless world
that called him citizen.

The Left, Summer 1931; *We Gather Strength*;
Proletarian Literature in the United States, 1935

HARLEM RIVER

by the huge dead yards
where freight trains wait
and brood, warehouses' vacant eyes
stare out at a world made desolate;
but the tugs *bloot* their egregious pride,
and the scummy waters twinkle with light.

they've suicided from this bridge—
ginks out of jobs, and the dames for love—
their peaked, pale faces rise in the dark
futile with yearning, tear-wet, stark:
i wonder what vast, dim dream of peace
they sought, in the susurrant waves' embrace.

night's breasts were soft, cajoling sleep . . .
her lewd eyes beckoned their weariness.
and now they are ground to the ultimate dust
that settles between red tenement bricks;
and now they are one with the particled past
siltering up weird, hopeless streets.

but high spires glow in the lonely gloom.
trains clatter and roar, and softly, laugh.
the pavements, endless in grim contempt
of hunger and lust, glitter like glass.
in the brief white glare of the smart arc-lamps
strange shadowshapes loom, and threaten, and pass.

New Masses, December 1931;
We Gather Strength

NICKEL-ARTISTS

(Editors' Note: Spector was one of 42 contributors to *Readies for Bob Brown's Machine*, published in 1931 at Cagnes-sur-Mer in the south of France by Roving Eye Press. Among the others represented in the volume were Charles Henri Ford, Eugene Jolas, Gertrude Stein, James T. Farrell, Kay Boyle, Norman MacLeod and William Carlos Williams. Included from Alfred Kreymborg were these "Regrets":

"Old man Kreymborg has grown too seedy

To write Bob Brown a speedy readie"

The concept behind the volume—and Spector's opinion of the results—are contained in his *New Masses* review reprinted here following his contribution.)

In this age of Wordies, we must contrive their mechanical means the Readies . . . but after the Readies, what?

it is simple.

we go the way of all flesh, towards spiritualization.

Take that new thingumabob, now, worked by waves of ether that are controlled and modulated simply by waving both arms or either, in an orchestral manner and producing substantially music for only 275 dollars: which price will suffer or enjoy a reduction, coincident with increased sales of the commodity, until: BE YOUR OWN MUSIC-MASTER—FOR THIS WEEK ONLY—$2.75—ACT NOW! as with music, also only more so, with thought.

simply consider what stuff lies buried within the folds of nickel-artists' convoluted brains,

absolutely impossible even for the wordie-birdie to exploit;

as the english sparrow lightens the labors of street-cleaners,

so the wordie-birdie makes freud fairly obvious . . .

and though with the Readie-tape the process of eating words is accelerated—that is not yet enough!

(sweet, clever capsules are the stuff!)

NOW WE MUST REALLY LOOK INTO THE FUTURE—

whew. brrrrrrr: 'tscold.

I seem to se . . . (hand me the globe Oswald,)

Culture growing in Leaps & Bounds.

Like a Grotesque Gazelle, like a Buttersnipe.

The World is so full of all manner of Tripe.

I see Words become anomalies.

The forest is obscured by Trees.

Artists in a Horizontal Pose

Manufacture out of Lethargies,

Unearthly Super-Works of Art.

I see the Whole become a Part

Of what the True Whole ought to be.

I see the forest in a single Tree.
Before the Artists, as they ly
In flaccid, fruitful Harlotry,
I see Machines, uncannily
Transform and store their Energy . . .
I can descry
The cultivated Monde, *en masse*,
Absorbing an almost edible Hash
Of Literature-In-The-Pig's-Eye.
In Times that are as Hard as these,
See BREADLINE-HEADLINES in the Papers, please-
It is not strange the Weaklings strive
To win a modicum of Ease,
And cannot Sleep soundly enough!
(Sweet, Clever Capsules are the stuff.)
In Cities, with their Guts of Steel,
We find it difficult to Feel;
Yet Yearn for Opiates: Howzat?
Perhaps we're Talking through our Hat?
(replace the globe,) . . .
(take care, you dope!)
I'm game to bet, in the Future woild,
Art will be Free as the Very Air;
And like the Air, a little pserled
By Nickel-Artists being there . . .

Readies for Bob Brown's Machine, 1931

THE INKLESS REVOLUTION

THE READIES FOR BOB BROWN'S MACHINE,
Roving Eye Press, Cagnes-Sur-Mer, France.

Pay attention, comrades. There are revolutions and revolutions. Some them, the literary ones, are taking place under our very noses, and we cannot even smell them. Or can we?

"Revolutionize reading", says the manifesto of Bob Brown, "and a Revolution of the Word will be inklessly achieved." The idea comes from Paris this time, not Rapallo or Riga and Bob Brown is the blushful inventor of a "reading machine" that will enable us to acquire culture at a very rapid rate, for "our potential consumption of words through all the senses is terrific," not to say terrifying. "Perhaps," says Brown, "words may be tasted and smelled someday in addition to being seen, heard and felt."

In an anthology designed to show you how it all works, Lawrence Vail obligingly lists some necessary bric-a-brac for the interior of any uptodate lunatic asylum, as follows: "farchitecture—moosick—mewsick—hooturism —rearalism—frothels—sinemas—not-abilities—sellabrittles—Krankusi— Androgydes—Ra-ra Ezra—Ritz Carlton Reedy," and others that must be consumed in order to be appreciated. Other contributors are represented, who put Gertrude Stein and the old *transition* gang to shame. Marinetti in Italy gives vent to: "Destruction of syntaxes. Wireless imagination. Geometric and numerical sensitivity. Words in rowdy freedom . . . It is she this fragrant highly nimble ovidal volume of cool pink milky perfumes with above 3, 6, 9 spirals of extract of vanilla," very alluring indeed in a country of Prohibition and AlCapon-ism. But I'll take mine with strawberry.

Bob Brown's statement of how he was converted to the "Readies" provides excellent clinical material for an understanding of the lives of these rootless, psychopathic expatriates. "I had to think of the reading machine because I read Gertrude Stein and tape-tickers in Wall Street . . . I've tried to explain to dullards before and it makes me mad if they don't understand . . . I wanted to be a great writer and a rich man . . . I was almost a book myself . . . The war came along and I did nothing about my machine except try to explain it to an occasional friend . . . For a living, I dealt in rare books. I bought (a book) for two dollars and sold it for fifty . . ." And now this tickertape-reading Mr. Brown, who can boast of having been a contributing editor of the old *Masses* (maybe *that* was what was wrong with it,) is intent on selling his "idea" to America's intellectuals. Harmless enough, you may say. But not if you understand the inherent viciousness of such "dilettante" tactics of evasion. Manuel Komroff, who represented one of the few dissenting voices in the anthology (the rest were the usual run of faded pansies, venomous fascists, thrill-hunters and defeatists, even including several misguided young "leftists" said: "And through it all—with the whole damn world convulsing in agony—through it all, you spit on your tin whistle and fife me a little tune that says no more than Yankee Doodle."

But if Komroff thinks that Yankee Doodle or the Reading Machine bear no relation to the contemporary struggle, then the previously mentioned Mr. Vail, in another of his orgasms, entitled "Progrom," has written in vain. He suggests that we "club lowly Loeb—manhandle Mendelsohn—pop off Oppenheim $ $ $ let Roth rot—rub out Rubinstein—jam Jews—kick Kike —gip Yit," and presently, after he has read this review, must surely add: "expectorate on Spector." Or perhaps, "krush Komroff." All of which is admirable self-exposure in a volume that purports to be "a preview of a revolutionary event in literature." Of my own contribution to the anthology I am much too modest to speak, except perhaps to say that the gist of my message is contained in two lines:

"as the english sparrow lightens the labors of streetcleaners,
so the wordie-birdie makes freud obvious . . ."

However, it is indeed a surprise, and a not very pleasant one, to find the following from the pen of Norman McLeod, former editor of *Front*, *Morada*, associate editor of *Left* and others:

"tomorrow-i-will-repeat-Red-orgiastical-with-padres—
calling-one-girl-to-another-in-midnight-confessional—
and-little-enough-the-seeds-springs-in-to-being-go—"

and from another editor of *Left*, Jay du Von, this riotiously juicy bit:

"BREASTS-CURVING and-now-DRUNK-with-IVANOV and-RAOUL-TALKS-of-mexico and-SHOWS-his RING . . . and-YOU-are-ASLEEP-in-my-arms"

Nerts . . .

New Masses, July 1932

(Editors' Note: This review by Spector was twice victimized by faulty typesetting/proofreading but it is conceivable that because of the nature of *Readies* nobody noticed. The Komroff quote appeared as (/denoting end of printed line): "through it all, you spit on your tin whistle and fife/ ing in agony—through it all, you spit on your tin whistle and fife/me a little tune that says no more than Yankee Doodle." The printed version also implied that Marinetti had done his own word tampering: "highl ynimble." The second reference to Komroff also transposed the "m" and "r.")

THEY WALK IN OUR SUN

They walk in the sun of our labors,
    on avenues we have paved,
They gleam in rich garments, and murmur;
    civilization be saved!
They walk in the sun of our labors
    and curse us, and call us depraved.

They lived in magnificent mansions
    whose stone we have wrestled in place,
They guzzle our blood, and graciously
    turn to spit in our face:
Culture's a product of leisure,
    and of that you have not a trace!

They grunt over tables of curious foods
    torn from our sinews and backs,
They've taste and discrimination,
    and, in a pinch, Exlax;
But we've only hunger and thirst: sensation,
    and we can be fed upon wax.

They're clever and cute to themselves, these folk,
    who wanted to preserve *status quo*;
They've got all the virtues you've never had,
    and others you'll never know;
Particularly they have got
    an awful lot of dough . . .

And they walk in the sun of our labors
    while we lurk underground;
And the world is very well ordered—
    as Columbus said, it is round;
And we have saved for the Bourgeoisie
    a suitable garbage-mound . . .

Some day, soon, your bones will rot
O smiling gourmands, glib and fat:
    we'll toast the proletariat—
    some day, soon!

The Rebel Poet, July 1932

100

KREYMBORG THE INFANT

THE LITTLE WORLD, by *Alfred Kreymborg. Coward-McCann. $2.00*

Alfred Kreymborg says sentimental things about a proletariat he cannot understand, and childish things about an economic system whose workings have never been quite clear to his beauty-fumbling, kindly eyes. If Kreymborg is to expand, he must cease being garrulous about trivialities, he must break with the rottenness of contemporaries like Pound and Williams and go toward the objective in a literary sense with the singleness of purpose that characterizes the efforts of men like Dreiser and Dos Passos. Making whimsical comments on social phenomena is not enough: *satire* is needed, the thrusts of revolutionary criticism. Whether Kreymborg is capable of this remains to be seen. So far he has done no more than scratch the surface. His reverence for "leaders" in the abstract causes him to utter nonsensicalities about Lenin and the social-defeatist Ghandi. He mildly rebukes the American capitalist, suggesting that, if he would only put more fodder in the dinner-pail of the workman, he would see "more blue in his eye, less red." This is political infantilism, and Kreymborg is old enough to know better. At any rate, a short course at the Workers' School would certainly help this poet in the better organization of his material, and some personal contact with the day-to-day struggle of the worker will give it the necessary illumination.

New Masses, July 1932

SADLY THEY PERISH

(A Dirge for the Objectivist Poets)

now in the perfumed dusk,
     a pause
the phosphoroscent worms emerge
like vacant, jangling trolleycars . . .
a purblind peace,
the gentry of the bourgeoisie
squirm into purple space.

5 years: the ivory towers crack,
the walls are eaten with decay.
the eliots, the ezra pounds
play jazztunes of profound regrets
in hideouts of expatriates . . .
"this is coming to you by remote control."
the sacred muse, an anxious cockroach, darts
here and there along the floor . . .

"oh death, where is thy sting?"
a rain of shrapnel in the streets:
clubs, teargas, speeches, bayonets,
the castor oil, the rubber hose,
the raids, the lynchings, pogroms, wars . . .
but butterflies have gauzy wings;
blue buzzards roost on empire-state.

confused, confused,
the images awry
like sappy roosevelt grins in coney-island twisted mirrors,
some little fanfare for the weird esthetic guy
    then shrugs and sneers,
applause that gutters to a hiss . . .
prince hamlet scrapes a violin,
wears rubber heels:
absorb the shocks that tire you out . . .

fascism yawns,
        black pit of death.
objectivists stuff cotton into ears,
disdain the clear emphatic voices of revolt
yet seem to hear, though dimly to be sure,
the ancient rocking-chairs of ease
creak absent-minded praise . . .
and pansy poets bow, and sway,
launch battleships and yachts of plutes
with girlish giggles and champagne salutes;
or else (thank-god) remember yesterdays,
fingering the junk of medals on their breasts . . .

sadly they perish, each by each,
whispering madness, they disappear . . .
into the isolate doom of dreams,
into the cold gray vaults of dust.
and who will gather the darlings up,
arrange them in anthologies?
what mussolini-horse will drop
bouquets upon their mouldering graves?

5 years: the ivory towers crack!
cockroaches scuttle after crumbs . . .
the harried line of workers holds;
repulsed, returns to the attack!
in trenches, behind the barricades,
electric eyes pierce walls of fog . . .
in arid wastes of no-man's land
white grubs squirm into purple space.

Partisan Review, June-July 1934

HOW OBJECTIVE IS OBJECTIVISM?

A review of JERUSALEM THE GOLDEN and TESTIMONY,
both by Charles Reznikoff and published at $1.00 by Objectivist Press.

Charles Reznikoff expresses in his poetry the limited world-view of a "detached" bystander: that is, of a person whose flashes of perception for the immediate esthetics of the contemporary scene are not co-ordinated in any way with a dialectical comprehension of the life-process. The artistic result in this case is a consistently minor body of poems, or fragments, none of which completely portray the object. Even so, it is easy to see that this poet is sensitive and gifted. His failure is not the failure of talent or method, which he labours ceaselessly to perfect. It is the failure of the Objectivist school of poets to which he still belongs. More precisely, it is the failure of the by-stander to comprehend the world.

In a semiconscious attempt to compensate for his self-enclosing attitude, the poet often returns to the past, to Judea, to the faded glories of the Jewish race.

"and God said, Be slaves
to Pharoah. And it was so."

Against the assaults of the present time he lifts the shield of fable and myth, not in the fashion of decadents whose naivete can no longer be sustained by any competent modern mind, but as one who is incompletely rebellious, who is apologetic and distraught at the spectacle of the breakdown of his class, who hesitates to view clearly the future. Reznikoff still smacks his lips over crumbs of the petty-bourgeois feast. That only crumbs remain is testified by the fragmentary character, as well as form, of his writings.

In *Testimony*, a book of rewritten case-histories drawn from legal sources, Reznikoff compels admiration for the finished restraint of his style, but again fails to reach artistic depths because of artificial limitations. Why do so many talented young writers insist on giving us bloodless imitations of the humorless bourgeois "great"? Louis Zukofsky, for example, has turned out to be nothing more than Ezra Pound's errand boy in this country, subordinating everything to the services of the Sacred Buttocks . . . The fatal defect of the Objectivist theory is that it identifies life with capitalism, and so assumes that the world is merely a wasteland. The logical consequence is a fruitless negativism.

But there is reason to expect that Reznikoff will soon cast off the frayed, starched-collar of Objectivism. He has already made significant attempts to contrast ideologies in *Testimony*. His brief poem on Karl Marx in *Jerusalem the Golden* is much more than an ornamental tailpiece to that volume. Profound world events cannot leave a poet of his integrity and sanguine temperament cynical or indifferent. He must soon realize that history permits him the alternative: either to succumb to the paralysis of reaction, or else to take that great step forward which is the way of revolution. Impartiality is a myth which defeatists take with them into oblivion. The creative man makes a conscious choice.

Dynamo, Summer 1934

MAY POEM

In the Spring the poets sing
About the bird upon the wing.
Upon my word that is absurd
Because the wing is on the bird.

Almanac for New Yorkers, 1939

OCTOBER POEM

When Dusk, a tedious Local, crawls,
Infinite shirtsleeves crowd the dusty sills,
And bulbs of Oberon appear,
Gilding all the pawnshop balls.

Almanac for New Yorkers, 1939

SPIN, LITTLE CHILDREN!

Midnight mutes the squalid slum,
Glimmering ghetto walls
Recede;
Slumped figures crawl,
Toil heavy feet,
Remembering scrolls of Israel. . . .

The neon-bracketed
      "Kosher Lunch"
Glows vivid as a jungle bird,
As in the arctic skies one star
Diagrams tenements asleep. . . .

What visions rise from conduits?
What waverings of steamy breath
Like whiffs in eyes these dim flats hold
Plunk through dreams as low viols?

The pseudogangster in a slantbrim hat
Spills lingo: swift, evasive, wise;
His finger jabs at enemies
Scrammed from the circuit of his braggart lies.
Impervious centuries stand and watch. . . .

They who conceive
In fetor, under creaking steps,
Whose eyes are viscid in this night
Flickering like carnivals,
Dream generations in a weary train
Clanking over blackened ties. . . .

Placenta twists about the brain;
They fold their arms on windowsills,
Gazing beyond the livid veil
At death's resplendent terminus. . . .

    Spin, little children, slowly whirl!
    Wan, hebraic in lament;
    Your limbs are in the cool not buds
    But shuddering trees in blackguard winds
    Sweeping across metropolis. . . .

Almanac for New Yorkers, 1939

SUNDAY ON THIRD AVENUE

This is that gray, dead holiday:
The world external, vacant,
And the brain careens . . .
An apathy descends upon the shuttered shops,
    the tattered screens,
Invades the tepid coffeepots,
Winds through a thousand furnished rooms,
Then flows in streams
    down gutters into sewer-drains.

Blurred windows gloze the hours that hover
Over a drunk's paralysis,
The swift delirium of a lover,
A pauper's thinly clawing fist . . .
Long trains that grind, and roll, and clamor
Lunge in a tropic slum of dreams
With rasping clank of horrid chains
And medieval mutterings . . .

The retrograde metropolis
Crumbles into glaucous mist
And lies along the tracks, remote,
Menacing no-one.
    We stand upon a platform; wait,
    abstract, intent,
    like sheep that huddle on a slope
    when, from afar, a storm is imminent . . .

It's late; long shadows ricochet:
Cold, draughty blocks grow desolate.
In igneous neon, strange words flow,
Liturgic, seeking gift of grace . . .
Now headlines, movies, comic-strips,
    What whirls between parentheses?

Impervious centuries stand and watch;
Reign absolute: morose, hard cops
Pounding the beat.

Poetry, February 1940

FLASH BULB

This is the secret falling of the snow—
Blue-white, green-white, beneath an ambience
Of areas of silence, and the glow
Of yellow lamps, in half-arrested trance.

This is the taxi, crouched and poised for flight,
Asthmatic with excitement of the chase;
Its plumed exhaust a symbol snatched from night—
The deathless dance of sprites in frozen space.

Now caterwauling claws the antique slate:
An El train, harshly coughing its complaint,
Reveals, in sudden blaze of sputtered hate,
This hackie, cowled in patience like a saint.

(Editors' Note: Spector's papers included a clipping of this poem from a yellowing newspaper page. He did not note the date or place of publication.)

TRANSPORTATION LORE

From YA GONNA LIVE AND DIE IN A CAB

—Bad business runnin' past them redlights. You know Pickles who used to save up cigarette labels? He got his that way: runnin' past 'em, runnin' past 'em, till he mistook one of the buoys in the East River for a corner-light, and ploppo! he nearly drowned to death.

—You know what they say, there's worms in apples and worms in radishes. Take the worm in a radish—he thinks the whole world is radishes.

—Like some fellow think if you get a colored guy for an icebreaker, you're skunked. I dunno, it never happened to me like that.

—Dames! They'll skunk you every time. Ride one for an icebreaker, and you won't book a thing all day.

—Say, did I ever tell you guys about the frail who says, call me a taxi! So I says, OK, lady, you're a taxi. So she thanks me profusely and walks away. Ha, ha, ha!

—Crise, it's all one family, ain't it, it's the same goddam tree. You wanna stick together, that's the only way to be. Otherwise you're gonna take a beatin'. There's different branches, but it's all the same goddam tree!

—Halfa what you eat keeps you alive, the other half kills you.

—Not alone you gotta live like a dog, they make a mongrel outa you. And then you gotta wag your tail. . . .

—Sure, they're fulla polite, these phonies. It's the bunk. I happened to cruise by the Hipp once, it was rainin' cats and dogs, so the wheel spills a little mud on a dame's dress. I'm Kid Galahad. I stops and offers to take her home, no charge. She steps in, and when I turns around, she says: Mount Vernon! I coulda spat in her eye!

—Whatcha say?

—I says, Lady, take the train if you wish and just sue the company. That's all.

—This ain't no occupation—it's a slavery proposition. You gotta mingle with everybody, take all kinds of abuse. If a guy's stuck, it's push me! If a lady's sick, take her to the hospital. Then go scratch for your money. Aw, you can't make a buck no more. . .

(Editors' Note: This piece, which appeared in the November 1946 issue of *New York Folklore Quarterly*, carried the joint credit line of Marion Charles Hatch, Hyde Partnow and Herman Spector. It was written when they worked on "Living Lore of New York City" for the Federal Writers' Project of the Works Progress Administration. The next piece, "Hacking New York," contains some of the same material and was published in 1954 in *Sidewalks of America*, edited by B. A. Botkin. Botkin, who directed the Living Lore project, identified the material as being collected by Hatch, written by Spector and Partnow, and specified that it came from manuscripts of the W.P.A.'s Federal Writers' Project, 1939.)

—Not unless you got a printin' press.

—You're a public servant. What can you do?

—The boys was tryinna be funny, so they got hold of this big police dog, I think it was Joe Schoenberg's, and put him in Sleepy's cab before he could catch wise, So Sleepy starts ridin', the dog's sittin' in the back seat, and a supervisor spots him. "Whatcha doing ridin' with the stick up?" He seen the dog's shadow, so he thinks it's a passenger. They begin to argue back and forth till the supervisor throws the door open. Then the dog jumps out and scares both of them outa their wits.

—Cabs is no place for dogs, believe me! I got a friend out in Brooklyn found that out. A lady calls up the office, you know they got those stations out there, and they send him over. He rings the bell, the lady hollers out, she's comin' right down, so he starts cleanin' up the cab. While he's got the door open, a dog jumps in, so he chases it and seen it run up the porch where there's another mutt. Just then the lady comes out, gets in the cab, and the two dogs jump in with her. He takes the fare to Bensonhurst, the lady pays him, and the dogs jump out and follow her. So he thinks nothin' of it. Next day the same lady phones the office, she wants a cab again. But don't send me the young man I had yesterday, she says. Wassamatta, anything wrong with the guy? Oh, she says, he's all right, only I don't like the idea driving with a feller who carries two dogs along when he's on the job. Can you beat it?

New York Folklore Quarterly, November 1946

HACKING NEW YORK

I.
COPS

—One of the boys goes in front of the judge and gets a dismissal. "What's the charge?" "Retardin' traffic." "Did you whistle or signal to him?" So Gilbright says, "I'm tired of all the time movin' my hand"—like that—"and blowin' my whistle." "You're a public servant. Case dismissed!"

—I run across a finagler last Monday. I was doin' a coolie over at the stand at Fortieth and Seventh. He pulls a thumb at me and says, "Get out of here quick and let this Packard in!" Luckily I seen him take a buck from the driver and stick it in his top pocket. So I says, "Nothin' doin', I'm stayin' right here. This is a public hackstand, ain't it?" So he gives me a ticket. "Okay," I says, "but you're goin' to the station with me right now." I tell my story to the Captain, and he makes out he don't believe me. "This is a very serious charge," he says. So I reach in the copper's pocket and pulls out the buck. Lemme tell you, that shut them up fast!

—Take one of these thick-headed coppers like Donovan. He's so dumb, if he found a dead horse on Kosciusko Street he'd have to drag it over to Gates so as he could spell it right on the ticket. Ain't that right? You know the guy.

—Talkin' about dumb cops. I got a friend Charlie, whenever they give him a ticket and they ask where he was born, he says "Czechoslovakia." So the flatfoot gets sore and says, "Keep movin', buddie, scram!"

II.
SCHMEGEGGIES

—I been on one identical spot, pretty near, for sixteen years, and I never seen it so bad. The longer you're in it, the poorer you get. You keep sinkin' and sinkin', like Sleepy up the line there. The guy never gets a good sleep in his life. I ask him, "What's the matter, Sleepy? Can't you grab some shuteye at home? The kids runnin' round the apartment, or what?" "Nah," he says. "It's me mother-in-law. Since she came to live with us, I gotta sleep on the couch, so I'm all broken up." That's why he's always rollin' up at the wheel. You hear about the time he gets a three buck call up on the West Side and stops on a light, and falls asleep? The lights change. All the cars is passin' him by. He's right in the middle of traffic. A cop comes over, and he wakes up with a snap. He looks back in the cab, and don't you think that fare took a powder on him!

—Here's what he done last week. Two old ladies give him a hail under the viaduct. They want to go to Pennsy. He's just after takin' a nap, so he rolls down Madison, turns over to Thirty-fourth, and there's the stream goin' north to the theater district. So he tails them around until he winds up right back at the Central, right on the line. Then he falls asleep again.

—What happened to the dames?

—Well he wakes up again, you know the way he does, like a stinkin' sentry, and here's these hens sittin' in the cab. So he scrams around the corner, figures, "To hell with everything!" When he comes back, they're gone.

—He's what you call a *schmegeggie.** But you got him trimmed a mile, aintcha, Barber? When a guy tells you "Tudor City," what do you do? You say, "What bridge do I take to get there?"

—Oh yeah? When they want to go to Canarsie, they always pick Maxie. All they gotta say is, "Waldorf Astoria," and he'll take them right out—to Astoria!

—So it happened once! There was lots of noise. I couldn't hear the guy. But how about the time you pulled in here with a yokel, a dame from out of town, and she asks you, "What's on the clock?" "Eighty-five, madame." Then she turns right around and says, "Why, driver, it's only thirty-five on the meter. Don't you think I can read? Ha, ha, ha!"

—"So what? What's funny about it?" I says. "if you knew it all the while, why did you ask me, lady? Tryin' to make a crook outa me for a lousy half a buck?"

—Trouble with you is, you're always ribbin' somebody. I won't even kid the shirt off a guy like Yonkel Stadium. What for? What's the sense?

—Somethin' screwy about Yonkel if you ask me. He's a fine feller but he ain't all there, if you know what I mean.

—That his right name, Maxie, or did you stick him with it?

—I don't rightly know what the hell his name is. He gets a call out to Yankee Stadium, the way I heared it, and the guy's green. He just don't know the joint from a hole in the wall, but he won't let on. So he keeps ridin' and trustin' to luck and lands up at Battery Park. So he breaks down and asks a cop, "Yonkel Stadium, where is it?" The copper has a good laugh, tells him how to get there, but by the time he makes it the game's over and there's eight bucks on the clock!

—Tie score! Yonkel didn't get there and the fare didn't pay.

III.

DAMES

—Dames! They'll skunk you every time. Ride one for an ice-breaker and you won't book a thing all day.

—Say, did I ever tell you guys about the frail who says, "Call me a

*Schlemihl, inept person

112

taxi"? So I says, "O.K., lady, you're a taxi." So she thanks me profusely and walks away. Ha ha ha!

—I happened to cruise by the Hipp once. It was rainin' cats and dogs, so the wheels spilled a little mud on a dame's dress. I'm Kid Galahad. I stops and offers to take her home, no charge. She steps in, and when I turns around, she says, "Mount Vernon." I could have spat in her eye.

—What did you say?

—I says, "Lady take the train if you wish and just sue the company." That's all.

—A lady calls up the office, in Brooklyn. You know they got these stations out there. And they send him over. He rings the bell. The lady hollers she's comin' right down, so he starts cleanin' up the cab. While he's got the door open, a dog jumps in. So he chased it out and seen it run up the porch where there's another mutt. Just then the lady comes out, gets in the cab, and the two dogs jump in with her. He takes the fare to Bensonhurst, the lady pays him, and the dogs jump out and follow her. So he thinks nothin' of it. Next day the same lady phones the office she wants a cab again. "But don't send me the young man I had yesterday," she says. "What's the matter? Anything wrong with the guy?" "Oh," she says, "he's all right. I don't like the idea drivin' with a fellow who carries two dogs along when he's on the job." Can you beat it?

Sidewalks of America, 1954

WORK PREVIOUSLY UNPUBLISHED

Living Folklore Introduction

The unpublished manuscripts, fragments and notes of Herman Spector show the third and final period of his writing career: the time when "he stopped sending it out for publication" as Norman Macleod said.

During the first two periods there were definite outlets for Spector's work, first the leftist literary magazines and then the assignments of the WPA Writers' Project. But, in the third period, the situation changed. He knew what he wanted to write and he worked hard at writing it but he didn't complete anything in a form he wanted to be published. And so he wrote, revised, destroyed or put aside for more work . . . and didn't submit. One speculates what might have happened if Spector, like Thomas Wolfe, had had a Maxwell Perkins to whom he could have delivered a trunk full of manuscript.

We know from family and friends that Spector destroyed most of what he wrote. Certainly nothing remains of his infrequent, unenthusiastic and unsuccessful attempts at potboiling short fiction for the popular markets. What does remain shows that he had in mind books on three subjects: one stimulated by his work on the WPA's "Living Lore" project, another on his experiences as a New York cabdriver, and the third based on his family and life as a boy and young man.

Portions of the unpublished work will be presented here in that order since, although he seemed to have worked on all three ideas concurrently once they were started, he probably initiated them in this order. It seems logical that the "Living Folklore" work began soon after the WPA experience and the hackie experiences began when he started driving a cab, although he had touched on the subject—from observation and probably from the experience of friends—while writing for the WPA.

The manuscripts from this period—unlike those from the first, which mainly are typed neatly in finished form with occasional handwritten revisions—survive in every form from tightly handwritten pieces on index cards or 3x5-inch pages torn from nickel spiral notebooks to typed 8x10 pages. All show the effect of heavy revisions which in some cases made the manuscript almost illegible. Wherever possible we are publishing the last revision. In some cases two versions are included and at times, which are noted, paragraphs which were crossed out in manuscript have been included.

At various times Spector considered "Living Folklore," "Streets of New York," "Kaleidoscope," "The X-Ray Eye" and "Coffeepot Characters" as a title for the work which follows.

POOR MAN'S OPERA

In a little alcove in the West Side Subway Station at 42nd St. there is a Seeburg Hi-Fi record-playing machine, jammed between a mechanical baseball game and a photomation machine—4 poses for a quarter, 2 bits. Painted in a sickly brown script on the plaster wall above the jukebox is the legend: "A Treasury of Immortal Performances." This is the poor man's opera and its devotees yield to no one in their rapt appreciation of the great voices and arias. Almost behind them in a sort of cul-de-sac are the sexy peepshows, poorly attended by comparison, though by equally devoted afficionados. Rare, mellow voices roll out those rich, Italian works of pain and passion. They ennoble this little corner of underground life.

A woman sits on a stool in the coffeepot concession opposite, gazes at these shabby, stubby little men who stand rapt in a trance before the magical sounds and she wonders what great stirrings work in their unprepossessing breasts . . .

STREETS OF NY

Here's a fellow with a geranium in his lapel and he's smoking a long, odoriferous cigar and getting ashes all over the flower. Some people can't even be trusted with a good smell.

Speaking of smells: What happened to those rusty, delicious herrings that came out of a barrel? Where are all the barrels—not only of herrings, but of pickles, of ripe red apples, of real sauerkraut? If we are forced to live in a plastic era, let them give us plastic stomachs, too, so we won't miss the real food we once tasted.

It was shape-up time on the pretzel front . . .

And where is the sweet-potato-man, and the roasted-chestnuts-man, and all those other trundlers of tasties and pastries? The only one I've seen around lately is the bagel-man. He had a lean, lost, driven look, and his eyes stared out, like glass immies on the empty, raw world at 3 A.M. He'll stick it out until the hydrogen bagel comes along and wipes us all off the earth.

My advice to you sweet young things . . .

CONCORD CAFETERIA
(Bridge Plaza Section)

An A.K.* hangout—where the weird meet to chomp their store teeth. A heavy yiddish brogue carries over the 2 for a nickel cigar smoke, which has tough competition in the clouds of woolworth perfume worn by dessicated hulks—they'll never give up the ship and oh, what a shape it's in! "Lena, you want hot mil,k or cold mil,k?" — "What kind cold mil,k?" — Romeo from Roebling St. likes his herring far from sober. He wears pinstripe blue pants (the stripes might be spaghetti), a pepper and salt jacket—it blends with the pickled herring—a green sportshirt adorned with a tie in which huge dabs of yellow, red, blue and white maintain a screaming independence. He may be advertising something, but he'll never sell it . . . A ponderous ex-blonde steps portentously over to the napkin counter, eyes the tinware malevolently, picks a few items at random while casing the joint for romance, then retreats to a table . . . The porcine girth's standard here; the norm is a caricature of the caricature of Boss Tweed . . . They toe outward, carry trays hidden under paunches. The floor, it will be noted, is of extra-solid stone . . . They gather together in chummy, gabby groups—in families, tribes, clans . . . Is it perfume, or disinfectant? . . . The intelligentsia here are water-drinkers and health addicts. They are much given to fingernail biting and leg twitching. This latter could be an unconditioned escape reflex. The nerves are willing but the flesh is weak. They'll never make it . . . Quite the contrary with these hefty Hannahs . . . the flesh is dead. You look for tattoo pictures on those huge, quivering slabs of arms.

*Alte Kocker—Yiddish slang for old-timer

A MEMOIR

I'd seen him often, on the street and off, alone or in the most diverse company; walking, loitering, driving. He affected casual but expensive sports clothing, a green tyrolean hat with a red feather in it, and imported shoes. At one time he'd be tooling up Central Park West in a brand-new foreign car with a theatrical-looking blonde at his side. Another time he'd be lurking in a Times Square arcade, in serious converse with a seedy faggott. Or drifting around the clusters of derelicts and frothing soapboxers in Union Square, listening or pretending to listen, his face a mask, his thoughts well hidden. What was he? Pimp? Undercover man? Probably a pusher. I grew curious and set out to learn what I could of this mystery character.

Because of his unvarying and fairly distinctive dress, and because of a certain comic irregularity about his features, he was easy to spot in a crowd. I discovered that his pedestrian movements followed a regular pattern. His beat began on the Bowery, continued to 14th Street, turned West along Broadway to Times Square, Columbus Circle, thence to a malodorous cafeteria at 72nd Street where a coterie of queens and fairies held court. This was the end of the circuit, and here he would remain until closing time, about 1 A. M., drinking coffee at a table with the aloof air of a baron at a country inn. The fags and other regulars knew him, it seemed, but approached him diffidently and addressed him with the respect due a man wielding some degree of power.

(Editors' Note: this is an alternate fragment):

A regular hanger-on at the 72nd Street Automat, that hive of faggots, is a mystery figure. He is a chappie of middling years with no visible means of support. I have seen him driving an expensive foreign car about town, talking with theatrical people and members of cafe society and loitering about subway stations with seedy pansies. What was he doing among these paupers? His nighttime beat was a drifting line that went from Union Square along 3rd Avenue to 42nd Street, west to Times Square, up through Columbus Circle, and along Broadway to this malodorous cafeteria. Because he constantly assumes the same dress, green tyrolean hat with feather, sport jacket, flamboyant shirt and shoes, I am able to pick him out from others on the street. I have seen him lurking in a subway arcade, hovering around a group of debaters at the edge of a square. I heard him in earnest converse, at an Automat table, with a chalky little gent who might have been a bellboy or an ex-jockey, or both, and heard scraps like? "Over at Eddy Denning's place," "The Hotel Seminole," and "how did Johnny get the black eye?" But the Tyrolean was blatta all the time; he never cracked out of form, never ventured a positive opinion. He might be a "pusher"; he might be a fag's patron; he might be a pimp; he might be anything—but nothing good.

OF OLD AGE, POVERTY AND
TWO PEDDLARS ON A HILL

Where do all these pathetic, poverty-pinched, elderly wanderers come from? They crowd the no-ticket cafeterias all over town, huddle in corners of trains at odd hours, drift aimlessly along the street, sigh and sun themselves on parkbenches. Not all are derelicts. When I see an old fellow, warming up a chair at the Automat, fold a paper napkin carefully and put it into his pocket, I think of my father in his last years, when he'd lost his business, his "friends" had deserted him, but he went "into the city" every day to do—what? To buttonhole former business associates and try to get a "connection" again. He was a great one for collecting those free Automat napkins.

Every day he would take the train and go "into the city" to "see the trade." He saw the trade, all right. He saw the busy-busy factories chopping

out ladies' belts, he saw the showrooms of samples and the machines that cut and sewed and fastened and pasted. And he thought of the times, long, long ago, when he was a factory owner and kingpin in this little corner of the world. He was President of the Ladies' Belt League which was an affiliate, or subsidiary, of the Ladies' Wear League. With all that Ladies' business, I once joked, he should have been a Ladies' man. But he was only a family man and a hard worker with a heart and a determination that nothing could down. Except an Old Folk's Home. That did it, for him. The day before he died, he told me: "I don't care to live anymore."

(Editors' Note: In the manuscript for the above, penned on an 8x10-inch sheet, "My Old Man" was replaced by "Two Peddlars On A Hill" in the title and "my father" in the text. The following, written on both sides of a 3x5 page from a spiral notebook, is probably an earlier—and certainly less personal—version on the same subject.)

There is a fringe population in New York of pathetic, poverty-pinched, lonely Elders. You may see them huddling in corners of the subway trains, holed up in chain cafeterias where they lengthen the coffee break out of all semblance, or drifting aimlessly about the streets. These are not derelicts I mean; they have a home of sorts, they do not drink, they are no humble examples for the hypocritical moralizers of the good life. They are, occasionally, trashbasket scavengers. They collect Automat napkins, free samples of cherry gum, circulars of all kinds. In the trains, they snatch newspapers, but often get beat out of the prize by those subway pros, the businessmen snatchers, who can sneak a paper deftly from some innocents while pretending to flick a speck of dust from their trousers.

THE X-RAY EYE

(Editors' Note: The following impressions were noted when Spector had one of his most hated jobs . . . as a door-to-door canvasser. He titled these notes "The X-Ray Eye" and intended that they include "Automat Sketches," "Bedford Stuyvesant" and "Bronx People.")

on a   in the bronx where grass grows sparsely is the moment of silence and ecstasy of one riffraff julip and his smudgefaced carmen

in an enchanted orchard behind an ancient house in Flushing lives a black rabbit with green eyes, and the tree in the front yard bears three kinds of fruit on the black branches; they fall to the ground to rot and no one enters the broken path behind the gate where low, twisting trees prevent any but an elf to pass . . . or a dog . . . yes, there is a fierce dog here. The squealing hag who controls him is rocking, creaking somewhere on the darkened porch. Inside the house is a feebleminded girl with terror inscribed upon her pink eyes. Her teeth are yellow, rabbitlike. She scuttles about in empty, mouldering rooms. One morning a dead, crushed sparrow is found on the rotted wide steps of the porch; the girl scoops it up, sneaks inside, tries to revive it but holding it next to her bony breast, the hag in the shawl becomes suspicious, tries to wrest her secret from her

in the fog and night all the streetsigns seem written in some ancient script, with flaring serifs all—that point the way to a wonderful past

as a drunk who lurches past the door of his own familiar home,
his violence and stupor habitual, forgiven . . .

the moon is a golden sliver in the down-fogged sky

it was brisk autumn, a fine time of year in the suburbs, a time to knock on strange doors and say hello.

in the rustic street, the poet-canvasser picked up acorns, leaves, pine cones, horse chestnuts, crabapples, and thought: this brick this lawn these trees this earth, its money, money, money . . .

In the dead, dull suburbs. At odd intervals, red coaches of the L.I. RR clutter by along the tracks atop that cindery rise; their chuff-chuff passage filling the deadened streets with acrid, black smoke; cloacal blessing on those shingled roofs. And sly disguise of aerials stuck up in disorder are the crown of thorns, the crucifix of human culture in this maddened age.

  Still, in the bare tree a bird still purls and chirrups. Still, although the sound is that of windowshades snapped, up, unreeling, flown out, and flapping. Still is this a link with the natural world: the world away from neurotic women and toadlike men who wallow in their moneyed rut. One takes a bit of comfort still from that.

DARK STREETS

Open the street door of any slum house and the first thing that hits you is the stink. In the vestibule, frozen dog-turd and gleaming splinters of glass from beer bottles. You can tell by the cooking odors who lives here. One whiff of bacon-fat and chitterlings and a strong odor of purple musk, and no need to read the names on the bells. They've been scratched out long ago. The boss won't let you sell to Negroes. You may as well skip this one. Hit the next house along the line. Hmmmn! Rice in a mess with tomato-sauce. Puertorican. Knock, knock. Que es? Only the old lady home, no peeka the ingles. Kids hop around without diapers or nether garments. The inevitable pottie under the bed . . . Here's a big kid, must be well over eight, wears long, unkempt hair like a girl's but due to the prevailing mode of undress, there can be no question which is which. So you wonder, and ask. Why the long hair like an Indian? The old lady tells you his mother has sworn not to cut his hair until he is ten. This is a "promise" made because he was born bald. Meanwhile he doesn't go to school, because the other kids would laugh . . .

OF PLACES

At the corner of Essex and Hester of an autumn evening, the air is clean, crisp, except where the odors of garbage lift from trickling gutters. Then you can smell the herring scraps, the rotten vegetables, everything that was sold and eaten in the neighborhood. A streetlamp spills golden tone on the black iron of the picket fence, on the pebbled pavement, on the sleek coat of a passing cat. A serious, spectacled girl hurries home from her courses at night college. A middleaged, broadbutted Slav comes by; his burly chest stuck out, his legs held stiffly, a painful dignity in his bruised face. Then an old woman, wise, grown slyer than a diplomat, choosing her way carefully. A lean mulatto kid just emerging from kiddishness, arcs a leg over a fire-hydrant as he passes. His shock of hair is defiant; his eyes glow with the need for some aimless adventure.

BENNY, A BLAHTTA BOY FROM BROWNSVILLE

At the Dubrow cafeterias—two in Brooklyn, one in Manhattan's garment center—you can study each small coin in the Smart Money mint. All the buttonhole magnates, bookies, pitchmen, managers, boxers, schadken, floozies, hoodlums, hackies and *blahtta* boys with no known source of income but plenty of sauce to their speech: pick your subject, sip coffee, and bend an ear. The gab goes on and on, circulates in and around each new arrival, drifts back and forth across the counters, and becomes ultimately recognizable as a milieu, a way of life. In the coffeepot army, Dubrovians are the generals.

The typical Male Dubrovian is a *blahtta* boy (whether in his 20's or 70's,) with a Broadway haircut, resplendent shoes, and sports clothes worn with a difference. The difference is that, to him, nothing is a sport unless he makes a buck on it.

(Editors' Note: Spector wrote two alternatives to, and expanding upon, the previous paragraph.)

The Dubrovian whose antics and speech habits are most representative of the milieu is between 30 and 50 years of age, flabby-male, overweight and

blahtta—worldly wise. His nails are manicured; he sports a "Broadway" haircut to prove he has hair; and wears sportclothes in and out of season. The latter provide the necessary Miami-Hollywood touch, proving the wearer to be no schnook but a character who has a buck or two and knows where to lay his hands on more. Cash is the sole criterion of sport as well as of any other activity. In the eyes of the Dubrovian, even wallowing about in sex would have no attraction for him if he couldn't spice it up with a little money-talk. "You shoulda seen de living room she ushers me inta," he boasts of a conquest. "Real pitchas on de walls, oils I mean, dey musta costed a couple gees each." When it comes to a really serious proposition like marriage, then a dame gotta be in the chips or it's no dice.

He chews a long cigar or a wad of gum, this afficianado of the Fast Buck, and is never at a loss for tidbits of gossip.

(or)

The "Dubrow-type", male, *blahtta*, age between 20 and 70, always exhibits the Broadway haircut (this takes hair!), gleaming new shoes, and sportclothes worn with a difference. The difference is that no sport unconnected with "making a buck" would have any standing in his eyes, and those which are so connected have never imbued him with the aficianado feeling, or elicited that athletic or muscular response which the free play of sporting instinct would seem to require. He usually chews gum, expectorates fluently and speaks fluidly. He wears a perpetual scowl, like he has just tasted something without ketchup, and hence can't recognize it as food. This is the visceral, non-intellectual type that Hemingway likes to study, along with the fish, as fisherman, the ageing torero, the weak-kneed tourist seeking thrills, and the always unprincipled soldier. The true Dubrovian, as I have named this dweller in a garish nether world, . . .

One such "blahtta boy", a sleepy-eyed, moustachioed, gaucho-y, elderly playboy, rides into Manhattan at the same time as I each workday afternoon. He wears the regulation sport shirt, his hair swept to a fashionable cut, and appears quite the conventional cavalier of kloak-and-suitery. The gnawing secret which he would rather die than reveal is that he too is a hackie. Among his fellow Dubrovians he passes as a stock promoter and race track plunger. These occupations are respectable; driving a cab is not. So he lives in constant dread of being caught some evening behind the wheel of a jalopy by an associate and relegated to some fringe-table at cafeteria head-quarters.

THE PORTRAIT

(Editors' Note: This fragment, subtitled "A Mystical Tale" by Spector, and "Nude with Violence" are starts on a short story using his own practice of drawing people he saw on the subway, in cafeterias and on New York streets.)

Eli Moll could never remember a name, but he had a marvellous memory for faces. Perhaps that was because of his hobby. Every spare moment he had, he devoted to sketching portrait heads. On little pads of paper, newspapers, envelopes, paper napkins—whatever came to hand. With practise he acquired skill and began to do things he considered not bad at all. Like the one of that old woman complete with babouchka, who rode the Brighton late at night when he came home from work. He'd had 3 or 4 stabs at it before he got it the way he wanted it. It wasn't easy. She had the patient, long-suffering face of a peasant. She was probably a scrubwoman in one of the midtown office buildings. Her hands were gnarled, her skin had the dull, viscous gleam of a pebble in muddy waters, her eyes were shards of kitchen crockery. He felt sympathetic to her at once, but realized it was mostly because she offered such an excellent subject for his swift crayon.

Eli was a lumpin drudge in the employ of a news company, but he might have been an artist. He didn't love the world any the better for that. Now, thirty-two, a bachelor, shy and friendless, he saw the evidence of spite everywhere around him. He sensed evil forces plotting to frustrate and direct him; at times their malevolence almost overwhelmed him. Lately, he'd heard a certain muttering . . .

NUDE WITH VIOLENCE

She had a middleaged face that was set into a mask of long-suffering patience. It was of an indistinguishable gray, the face of a scrubwoman. Nobody in the jogging, weary train gave her a second glance.

Nobody, that is, except the skinny, long-maned fellow sitting all hunched up in a window seat at the tail-end of the car. His muddy brown eyes flickered with interest as he looked up from some scrawls he was making on a large white pad and spotted her, placidly sitting with gnarled hands crossed on her lap, facing him. Covertly, diddling with his pencil, he studied her commonplace features. There's character in that face, he said to himself. The way her cheekbone rose and lost itself in the planes of eye-socket and skull fascinated him. The strong brow, serene and wide. The jaw whose line was subtly soft, yet determined for all that. The crockery eyes, too tired for laughter, too honest to hold gloomy secrets. Honest, open, sad eyes: he liked that. He hoped she was never merry or coarse. Just this way, with babushka on her graying head, she was perfect. The perfect peasant.

Swiftly, and without appearing to do so, he made a rich-black rendering of the image evoked in his own mind by that rough-hewn face. Indicated a value here, a tone there. The graphite pencil coursed and sped, turned and returned like a purposeful fly in his hand. He'd been doing these subway portraits for years.

For years and years, he thought, and what did it all add up to? Waste and futility. Working nights in a damned stinking cafeteria kitchen, swabbing up, pushing a clean-up wagon, taking guff from a fatslob boss. All because he had considered it prostitution, ten years ago, to plot out lettering for advertising signs. Or push a squeegee across somebody else's stencil. Now he was breaking thirty and nobody wanted him. His sketches lacked polish, lacked finish, they said. And he wouldn't take the kid salaries they offered. Not now, curse them! He tried to throw off the bad mood that had come over him. A mood like that made it almost impossible to draw, to see things *right*.

A jerking of the train made the woman shift in her seat, and she turned her head to survey the car. Then she turned back, and caught him drilling at her with hungry eyes. Almost automatically, she touched her plain gray hair under the babushka, primly smoothed her skirt down over the knees. If it hadn't been for that, he would never have noticed those legs. But he did, and almost gasped. They were the most lovely and voluptuous legs he had ever seen. They had no right to be there! They were wrong, out of character. He was indignant, but the sweep of feeling that made his nostrils flare now was not indignation. He would never admit what it was . . .

One reason Alex Mole had buried himself in a menial, wearying job with no future, no money, and no opportunities for social life was a great fear of women. The other reasons, rooted in complex psychopathology, were

subsidiary, and needn't concern us here. It was that great surging monster, Sex, that harmless toy dragon or tame lapdog to the well-adjusted mature citizen of our republic, which bugged him. The thirty-year virgin thought to exhaust himself each night and so avoid temptation. That is why, in his art, he drew faces, only faces. That is why he avoided contemplating younger women, and sought models for his pencil among the middle-aged and elderly. And that is why, confronted with an unexpected view of fine female legs, he felt as if, somehow, he were being mocked by Satan. As if his vows were being tested, the voluntary, unschooled vows of a solitary ascetic. He stared hard, frowning, calling upon anger to win the silent battle. And the char-woman in the babushka sensed this new warmth, this sudden and unusual regard. But misinterpreted it. She, too, felt stirrings, honestly admitted ones. She knew herself still a woman, still the cynosure of greedy eyes. Leisurely, almost kittenishly, she crossed the left leg over her right knee. Let the young man get his kicks, she didn't mind. Looked like one good night in bed with a lively filly would make him or break him. She sighed. Even twenty years ago, she'd be glad to put him to the test. Now it was just work, eat, sleep and pay the rent for her. Nothing to look forward to. Not even a bit of fun . . . She glanced out of the window and saw nothing but scratching blackness.

The train reached 28th Street when Alex came to a decision about the woman. Somehow, he must resolve this dichotomy of face and body. *Body?* He sought eagerly for hints of form beneath the unstylish, thick bag of a coat. Despite the heavy lines of the chin and neck, she showed no spread of hip or belly. He wondered wordlessly if the legs were but a fair sample of other youthful charms. Then he saw that she had uncrossed her legs and was making those little movements of imminent departure which signalize the experienced traveller. She would be getting off at 23rd Street, he thought. No, she musn't escape him. Casually, he replaced the pencil in its sheath, tucked the pad between the sheets of a folded newspaper, and reached the car door before she did.

NINTH AVENUE BAR

Ninth Avenue at night is a liquid glowing of stores and streetlamps. The wind that noses from the river carries an odor of dried fish and soggy vegetables. In the windows of a Greek grocery store, bottles of Grenadine and Tamarindo gleam; great wheels of black-hulled Romano cheese, with gold medallions of merit stamped on their sides, tower above cans of halvah, honey, antipasto, and olive oil; strings of figs hang from the ceilings; stiff filets of Pakayarro and Tsiros are spread out like riffled cards. Next door, in

H. Spector

the Salumeria, all shapes and sizes of sausage, salami, balogna hang in loops from hooks. A hockshop flaunting its secondhand bargains looks like a soused floozie making a play for another drink on the house. The hardware shops are all glitter-glatter. Plastic dresses sway in a belly dance outside the dry-goods store. And high in the sky, a long bright beam of light pokes through the purple mist to reveal where clouds whirl slowly.

Sheehy's is eternal New York, an ancient and respected joint that scorns to provide television. Here the only distraction is liquor. No loud talking, bumming around, or flirting with broads is permitted. A deer's head, stuck up on the wall above the mirror, proves that some of the boys have gone out of the neighborhood to do a little legal shooting. A silvery print, somewhat stained by the smoke and moisture of years, hangs on the rear wall under a lattice-work arch. It is a photo of the establishment as it once was. Except for the swinging doors, it is much the same today. A thin old gent with dewlaps and splotches of red in his face presides over the bar. This is Sheehy, the man himself.

A massive dame enters with firm step and sits at the bend of the bar, in the rear, like a grand lady settling into her manorial chair. She wears an oldfashioned white boa and sports a starved-looking mutt at the end of a leash. Sheehy doesn't mind a dog or two, if necessary. In the case of the big, nondescript dame, it's necessary. She will definitely get blotto tonight, and nobody but the dog is going to lead her home. She orders a boilermaker, and coughs discreetly. Sheehy sets a glass ashtray before her. She is daintily lighting up a perfumed cigarette. He winks at the dog, who doesn't respond, and returns to his discussion with a couple of oldtimers down front.

"What has 4 legs and flies?" asks one of the cronies, a railroad man living on his pension and social security. The other guy shrugs. Sheehy knows the answer, but pretends not to. "A garbage wagon," explains the quipster, and laughs loudly. The others merely smile, but the elderly little Italian who makes the sandwiches and mops up the joint for a pittance laughs with rare sincerity. He keeps laughing right into the next joke, which he doesn't understand at all, so he retires to the tiny kitchen alcove to examine the stock. He chucks away a stale butt-end of bread and salvages some stray hunks of salami for the soup. His face is now deadly serious . . .

NINTH AVENUE

Ninth Avenue glows with a festive air. The roped necklaces of bulbs in front of stores crammed with good things, the winking of red and green signal lights, the figures that appear and disappear about bright corners, all make the night seem like a scene in a play witnessed in some happier time. A play about little people in funny clothes living out their funny little lives.

A fish-stinking wind blows up from the river, bellies out housedresses in racked display, knocks a battered hat from an old man's hand, whips at the skirt of a pantherish beauty, whisks papers across the littered road. The wind is jocular tonight.

Here a hardware store glitters with gadgets. There a Greek grocery reveals: gleaming bottles of Grenadine and Tamarindo, great black-hulled wheels of Romano cheese with gold medallions stamped on their sides, stiff filets of fish, smoked and salted, strings of figs, and countless cans of halvah, honey, olive oil. A hockshop, like a twobit floozie leery of the cops, shows dusty bargains with a furtive air. And, high over everything, a searchlight's beam pokes through purpled mist to the clouds.

PUERTO RICAN HARLEM

The street is a swirling current (rapids) that breaks against the curb, or the store-front; rushes to converge in a whirlpool at the corner. People are driftwood, bark, insects, monsters; they skate upon the glassy surface, they lunge and heave with the tides, they wear brightly-colored clothes for sails. Then they spin in shifting currents and are lost to sight . . . Amigo! A nutbrown, wrinkled dishwasher greets his longlost bosom-pal, old playmate in the sanjuan slums. All around them harlem's kids, bouncing balls, they repeat the lives of their elders, their adjustment to slums, dirt, stone.

PANHANDLERS IN PURPLE

An elderly, shabbily dressed couple are peering into the warmly lit window of a restaurant around dinnertime: can you resist such a pitiful sight? No, not easily. You stop dead, watch a moment, feel in your pocket for a coin and then slip it into the old man's pocket. Shamefacedly, you may even murmur something appropriate to the faded but brave little creature standing at his side. She looks a little like your mother in the half-light . . . They've been around 42nd Street for years, this couple. Always work the gag at the dinner hour. It's a great act. And the stage setting: "Night, the City," makes it really socko.

The nighttime panhandler seems always more ominous, or more pathetic, than the guy who works the day shift. A figure waving its naked stumps at you in a dark street has what the ad boys call shock appeal. Panhandling can be an art which some moochers have gone to great pains to perfect. They don't just sneak up on you and stick out the grubby palm. That's for bums. The panhandler with pride develops his own specialty, plus a line of chatter to go with it, Usually he works the gag so that *you* approach *him*, not vice versa.

One night, very late, I parked the cab along 8th Avenue, near 57th, and prepared to take a coffee break. I was checking the cash intake, riffling the bills and clinking the coins in my changer, when I looked up to see an old fellow lean against a building and gasp for air. He was, from all appearances, a solid citizen: well dressed, physically well set up, suffering only some temporary disability. As he continued to lean and breathe heavily, I approached and asked if there was anything I could do to help.

"No—I'll be alright—in a moment," he gasped. "It . . . gets me sometimes. Asthma. Can you—help me—to walk? . ."

I helped him to walk but, unfortunately, also helped him to talk. He told a very sad and involved story, replete with authentic detail and chock-full of logic. It was a businessman's tale, and as I reflected later, it took a good con man to tell it convincingly. Certainly it deserved more than the single buck I was able to persuade him to take from me. All the classical elements were present: the stranger in the city, the business venture that failed, the crooked partner, the stolen wallet, and the day-long wandering about in a daze. Too much, too much. But what clinched it was the night, and the thought of that cold, dangerous park bench . . .

The very next night, hacking 57th Street, I saw this poor old gent leaning against Carnegie Hall in the same, sad condition. Somebody else was leading him and listening to him. I saw him reluctant to accept the handout, finally taking it with a dignified bow and bravely walking off. Afterwards, I caught his act on Broadway, that street of wiseguys. He went over big there. He had them choking down sobs. For months afterward, I spotted him here and there along the New York City circuit, always well-dressed, always in temporary distress. Then he vanished from the scene. Chicago, here I come!

MY WAR WITH THE CAR WIPERS

Now that all the Bowery El pillars are down, the familiar Car Wiper, a species of leathernecked, grimy, lurching grackle that lives exclusively on King Kong, has been deprived of his natural camouflage. Hasty-minded conservationists are already predicting his swift extinction.

True, the outlook is bleak. Mass migration to Brooklyn or the Bronx, it has been pointed out, where sturdy mid-road structures still stand, will avail him nothing. No borough outside Manhattan affords the same natural advantages of contiguity to fleaspecked bars, two-bit flophouses, and a sufficiency of human hosts to mooch from, or off. But what are all these worth without a base of operation? Forced into the open, he must contend with powerful enemies. Marauding autos and cops with unobstructed views will take their deadly toll. Wind and storm will rage unopposed. Even sunlight will sneak through in an effort to desiccate pickled flesh. It looks *blech* for the crumb-bum with the greasy rag. He may be compelled, ultimately, to use that accessory for its original sanitary purpose, namely, to wipe the schnoz. A gloomy prospect. He might just as well be dead.

Hope revives, however, when one considers the tremendous agility of this creative fellow. I regret the passing of this pest who, for years, has proved a fencer worthy of the finest thrust of my taxi. Always capable of great manoeuverability, he has compelled me to lunge and parry, back and fill, swerve and brake to a short stop, all to avoid his outstretched claw. Many a time I have strewn the cobbles with hard-earned coins as a foil for a getaway. Of course, I realized that money alone is not the objective but only a

134

side-issue with this ubiquitous cadgerer; what he is really out for is *victory*. Even so, I was not permitted to escape unscathed. "Afraid of me, ya louse?" And I'd feel the cynic sneer of my passenger, a dime tipper almost invariably, sticking in the back of my neck like a stiletto. The ride over, it would be a nickel gratuity for myself, and no retort to make. How could I squawk, when I'd just proved myself either a sucker or a skinflint? Anyone who truckles to a belligerent panhandler is, ipso facto, a sucker, in this town. Just as anyone who doesn't is a lousy skinflint. It's a dilemma, please.

My first brush with the dabbing specialist (alt., jalopy polisher) came when I was a rookie Hackie. I was tooling blithely down the Bowery at what I considered the optimum speed of 60 mph. It was a dark, wet night, I was skirting the trolley tracks, but all these portents were to me as naught. The only thing I cared about was finding a passenger to go with my nice new meter. I wasn't troubled about how many pieces I found him in. Just as I reached the cluttered intersection of St. Mark's Place, something lurched from behind an El pillar and aimed itself at me like a nike with a six-day beard, including overtime. I had just enough presence of mind to touch the brake and twist the wheel in all directions. The cab described a parabola while my eyes were still closed. Upon opening them, I found myself on the other side of the intersection, headed uptown. I stared. The bristly bozo who had caused this reversal was sitting peacefully on my left fender. With a rag, he calmly dabbed at the window. I closed my eyes again for a second, but when I suddenly opened them he was still there. I didn't dare to ask how, but I knew he couldn't have done better if he'd paid a quarter on the Coney Island Whip. After making both sides of the front window completely opaque, he tackled the butterflies. I don't mean the ones in my stomach, which fortunately were hidden from his view.

When he was completely satisfied, he held out a mottled paw. I placed a quarter in it, and he scuffled off, like some monster of the ocean's floor. Half-way across the road, he turned and winked: "Better get them brakes relined, Buddy!" And with one hop, he boarded the fenders of another auto, and was hurtling down to Chatham Square.

Once I knew what and whom I was up against, the battle was joined. I found that these birds work equally well alone or in pairs. More rarely, they will team up as a trio, and then the poor auto driver has no chance at all. They can station themselves in his front, rear, and at the curbside. For appearance, they can be highly deceptive. Apparently decrepit, they nevertheless scurry about, flop over, and leap into the air with the dexterity of a Harlem cockroach. The only casualty I saw was a poor, busted-horn specimen who'd been unlucky enough to tangle with a Jersey driver. Somehow, he'd never learned to watch out for Jersey license plates. Nobody wins against the Jersey driver. Believe me, I know. Not even a Bowery car wiper with his pavement-to-pavement leap.

A SYMBOL IN THE NIGHT

In the ugly city, this sadness too is ugly. The rumors of crimes, the frozen shrieks of victims, haunt these lumps of stone. Shadows pooling the hallways, the dead windows, the secret driveways, are cold with menace. The streetlamp is a searecrow to scatter furtive joys.

There is little laughter in the city at night, and not much to laugh about. But we manage a chuckle now and then. Once, in another city, I looked out of the window of my dingy hotel and saw far down the long, long night of empty stone a huge red neon sign. It said

         D
      H O T
         N
         U
         T
         S

The sign seemed to light up the entire sky. To me, a stranger alone in an unknown town, it was an invitation to warmth and friendship. I went downstairs and walked toward it. I passed empty block after empty block, the only sound I heard was the clicking of my own heels, and the sign remained high and huge and far away as ever. I was then a good walker, a veteran of long hikes in the stone forests, but I was weary when finally, I stepped into the sidewalk pool of light reflecting the neon sign. This was the edge of town

—beyond lay empty lots and railroad tracks. Beneath the sign there was a dimly lit cubicle of a store containing a counter on which were piled pasteboard boxes, a doorway leading to a dark hall, and nothing else. No stools for customers, no customers, nobody behind the counter. Who runs the joint, I wondered. Who comes way out here to buy hot donuts? Where are the donuts? And why this tremendous, Times Square neon sign to advertise a 2 x 4 joint? There was no answer, not only because nobody was around to answer, but because there could be no answer. This was the symbol of a civilization untouched by human hands. So what? So either shriek in despair as any other victim, or roar with laughter.

A DIME AND A DIME AND A DIME
(the old door-opener at
Grand Central Terminal, Lexington side)

The face is small and lean and ridged—a tight mask through which small gray eyes glitter fiercely. He chews tobacco and spits fluently, with skill or luck enough to miss the hurrying passersby. He is closer to 70 than 60; his shoulders are bowed, and he holds his hands in the secure pockets of his old black chauffeur's coat, liveried with a sprig of green paper and fold of stained handkerchief in the breast pocket. He wears a peaked chauffeur's cap. —Say, hackie, you got a screwdriver or bottle-opener on you? That middle door; they keep pushing it and it's locked. The news guy likes to lock it and I can't get it open with my fingers. No, you don't carry no tools with you? When *I* drove a cab, I used ta carry a bottle-opener all the time. Came in handy whenever I wanted a bottle of beer. Sure, I drove a cab in this town when they was only 4 cylinders.

—Work here 7 days a week. All I get is tips, when I get them. Been here since 3 o'clock this afternoon (now midnight) and I haven't raised a dollar yet. Should have a dollar and a half in my pocket by this time. I stay at a nice hotel in the Bowery, it's 60¢ a night, with carfare that makes 90¢. I got no expenses now, my boy's in the Navy. He's no trouble. No, I don't talk to nobody in the hotel. Got my own room, same room every day, go out and get a bottle of beer, save money that way you know. You get a nickle back on every bottle. Last week I was broke. Reached under the bed and counted 8 bottles. Took 4 of them back to the bar where I bought them, then took 4 more. Had plenty of carfare then. Good hotel, make my own bed, anytime I want fresh linen they give it to me. Oh, it's a nice hotel. These guys sit around the lobby are a bunch of—scuse me—cheap sons of bitches. It's a dime and a dime and a dime. That's the trouble—always lendin'. They never go out and work for a nickel or a dime like I do. One guy on the same floor

137

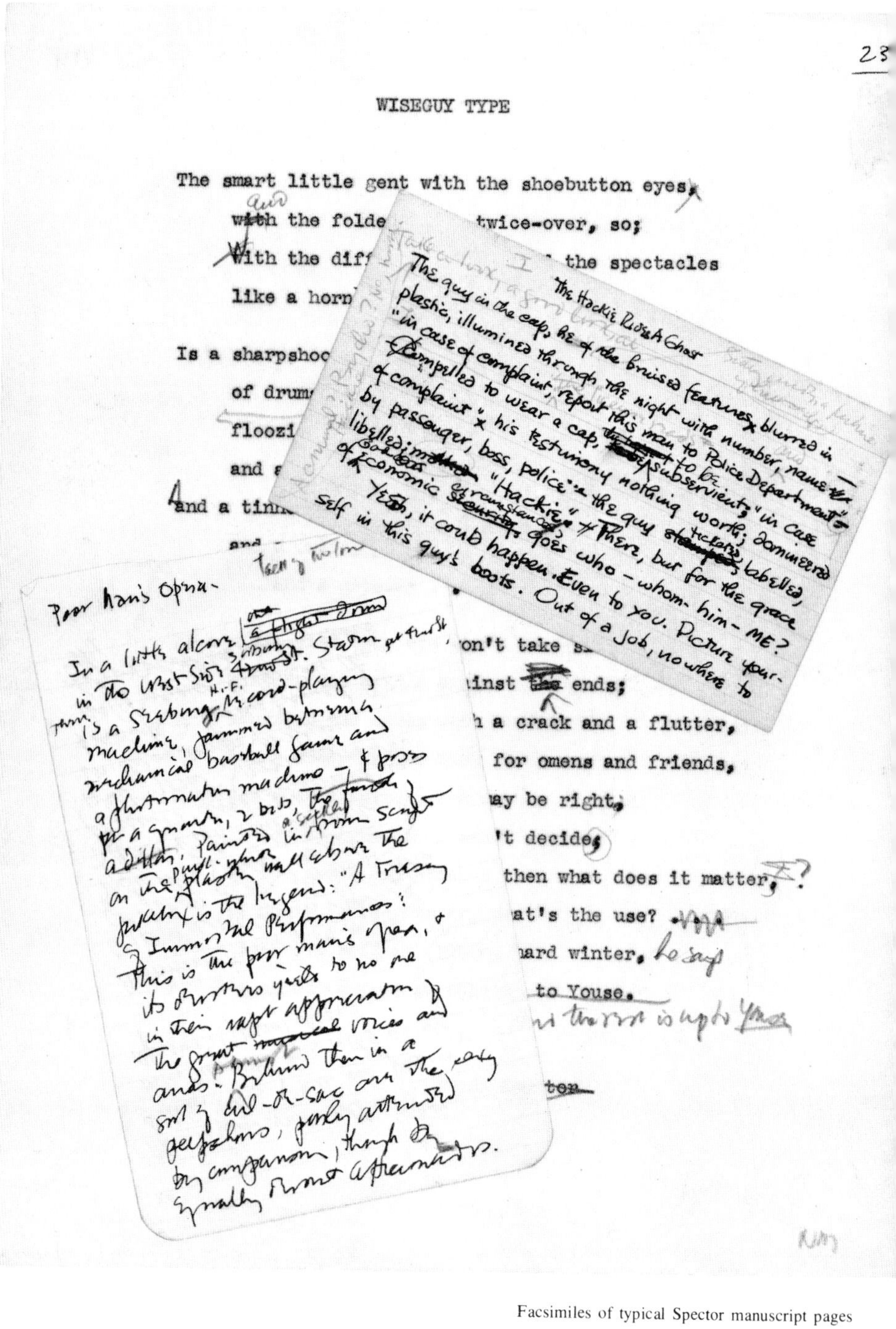

WISEGUY TYPE

The smart little gent with the shoebutton eyes,

    with the folde   twice-over, so;

With the diff   the spectacles

    like a horn

Is a sharpshoo

    of drum

    floozi

    and a

and a tinn

and

(overlapping handwritten manuscript note, partially legible:)

The Hackie Rides a Ghost
The guy in the cap, he of the bruised features, blurred in plastic, illumined through the night with number, name "in case of complaint, report this man to Police Department" compelled to wear a cap, to be subservient, "in case of complaint," his testimony nothing worth; ticketed, labelled, libelled by passenger, boss, police — the guy of economic circumstance. "Hacking" goes who — whom — him — ME? Yeah, it could happen. Even to you. Picture yourself in this guy's boots. Out of a job, nowhere to

(overlapping handwritten note, lower left, partially legible:)

Poor Man's Opera —

In a little alcove in the West Side, storm get first, there's a swabbing record-player machine, jammed between a mechanical baseball game and a photomat machine — & press for a quarter, 2 bits, the finest arias, painted in some script on the plush-glass wall above the jukebox is the legend: "A Treasury of Immortal Performances": this is the poor man's opera, & its glories yield to no one, in their rapt appreciation of the great musical voices and ands. Behind them in a sort of cul-de-sac are the early jukeboxes, poorly attended by comparison, though by generally moved afterwards.

(typed lines partially visible beneath notes:)

on't take   inst   ends;

h a crack and a flutter,

for omens and friends,

ay be right;

't decide

then what does it matter?

at's the use?

ard winter, *he says*

to Youse.

ton

knocks on my door. I open up. Whaddeya want? Can ya spare a dime for a
cuppa coffee? I give it to him. Never works. Next time same thing. Next time
he catches me goin' to the toilet. We got a big toilet there ya know. O, they
got nice accomodations in my hotel and he asks me do I want a drink. I know
what that stuff is, alcohol and colored water. No thanks, I says. So I give him
another dime anyway, he swears he's gonna pay it back. Think he ever did?
So last night again, knock—knock! "Can ya spare a dime?"—"No!" I don't
even get up to open the door.

Wanna know why I don't go over the West Side to catch the theatre
crowd? I'll tell ya. They got a click over there, and I think they pay off the
cops. First thing you know, they don't like you, you'll wind up with a black
eye. I tried it once, sure, but everything was taken. No, I been here for years
and here I'll stay.

WISEGUY TYPE

The smart little gent with the shoebutton eyes
    and the folded nose, twice-over, so;
    with the diffident smile, and the spectacles
    like a hornèd owl, so wise, so wise,

Is a sharpshooter born in a cabaret to a rattle
    of drums and a spastic shudder;
    By a pinkish floozie with powdered thighs,
    and a monocled punk in a cutaway,
And a tinhorn song, and a clicking jig,
    and a swift, pat fade
        and a getaway . . .

Is a wise, wise baby who won't take sides,
    playing the middle against the ends;
    shuffles the cards with a crack and a flutter,
    looks sharp in the dark for omens and friends,
Concedes with a mutter, You may be right.
    It may be true but I can't decide,
    If the cards are stacked then what does it matter?
    If death is the answer, what's the use?
I'm a lonesome wolf in a cold, hard winter, he says
And the rest is up to Youse.

(Editors' Note: Spector's typescript of this poem bore the penciled notation 'NM' which he used
to indicate *New Masses* but apparently this was never published.)

Call Me Porkchop   Introduction

The last 10 years of Herman Spector's life he was a New York cabdriver who thought of himself as a "porkchop," the cabbies' term for one of their clan who was "harmless but pitiable."

Much of this period Spector did no writing and nothing he wrote during the decade was published. Much of the writing he did was a continuing effort to turn his cabdriving servitude into a book. Uncertainty about its direction—many of the remaining manuscript fragments indicate that he thought he should try to be humorous when in fact he was bitter—show again how he would have benefitted from a competent and confident editor.

An outline which survives shows that Spector thought the book might be a "hackie case-book . . . 1st person narration, episodic, jocular, factual with interspersed elements of fantasy and fiction . . . hackies' tall tales . . . description of NY places and people . . ." His outline called for 11 chapters: "Penn to Grand," "Never Ride a Drunk!," "Sex Among the Canopy Tribes," "On Lingo," "A Stranger in the Bronx," "Crime Is Of the Essence/The Hoods," "Harlem Is Bad News," "Will It Rain, Driver?", "The Injured and Insulted," "Nobody Makes An Honest Buck" and "Lament for a Porkchop/Operation Porkchop." Although various notes show he thought of many prospective titles he seemed always to come back to "Call Me Porkchop."

Ironically, the last two publications of Spector's work during his lifetime were of pieces he had written about cabbies for the Federal Writers Project "Living Lore," some 10 years before he first drove a taxi.

And one of those was titled, "Ya Gonna Live and Die in a Cab."

CALL ME PORKCHOP

(Editors' Note: Spector thought of beginning this with an envoi or proem on "Night and the Hackie." Three versions—the first two leading to "Here I am in the gangster's cap . . . ." and the third to "I wore the gangster's cap . . . ."—follow.)

I am a night worker who sometimes has daymares. A nightowl Hackie, that stereotype of columnists and nite-clubbers referred to in jest. A pariah of a pave, a modern-day rickshaw coolie with rearview calluses and cannibalistic concepts. This is the image of myself that recurrs in the terrifying dream. When I wake, I know the dream to be a reality.

(or)

Sometimes the image of myself, a reflection of the stereotype view of spiteful journalists and upperclass snobs, becomes unbearably terrifying. Then I have a fearful dream. I dream that I am a hackie.

I am a nightowl Hackie, again. At times I feel like a pariah of the pave, a modern rickshaw coolie with rearview calluses and cannibalistic concepts.

(or)

I was lost in the deep, black night and dreamed a fearful dream.

I was a Hackie again, a pariah of the pave, a rickshaw coolie with rearview calluses and cannibalistic concepts.

Here I am in the gangster's cap, shiny-bottom pants, wearing the torn and eggstained jacket prescribed for all my tribe. A pencil is stuck behind my ear; my belt sags with the weight of a fully loaded nickel-clicker. I am obese, greasy, semi-literate.

Just over my skull, as I sat chained to the wheel like some galley slave to his oar, hung that badge of infamy, my Hack License. It resembled the tin nameplate stuck on the bars of a cage in the zoo, informing visitors of the genus, species, age and date of capture of the beast within. Mine was more detailed. Illumined in blurred plastic through the long night, it showed a cynical version of my phiz, gave my private name, public number, and warned:

> PASSENGERS For your protection keep a record of above name and number. Refer complaints to a Policeman or to Hack License Bureau, 156 Greenwich Street, New York City.
>
> POLICE COMMISSIONER

Apparently, I was dangerous. . . .

In the dream I drove on and on like a man demented through a night that was deeper than terror, madder than lust, stranger than metaphor. The

Passenger, a malevolent figure, squatted at my back, faceless, unseen, and constantly expelled noxious fumes down my neck. At times there would reach me a whirring, mechanical noise, like a cheap toy's windup:

"To the Plahza, plee-uz!"

Or: "You coulda made that light, Mac."

Occasionally, I was appealed to by some desperate wretch: "Please, hurry, driver, I'm two hours late already!"

The voices merged into each other and I heard a scream that dwindled and became a boozy mutter of rundown music when the juice is turned off the record player. Not once, during the seven years of my dream, did I work through the dawn, or see the rising sun, or the face of my Passenger. (Alternate version of this paragraph from Spector's manuscript: The rest was a psycho's dream, a boozy high, a rockroll giggle. And much maudlin muttering when the record ran down or the juice was turned off, and the lights went out and it was dawn again. Not once, during the seven years of my dream, did I work through the dawn, or see the rising sun, or the face of my Passenger.)

I developed a tin ear. All that clicked in my head were the names of streets and the numbers of houses. I said "Thanksalot" and "Watchyerstep,"

passenger from
the Waldorf

took heed of signal lights, growled back to the horns. All the horns were angry. I swore, and spat, and slavered, tugging at the leash.

To the Passenger, by whom I was paid, tipped, and swiftly forgotten, I was no more than a blind and muck-laden creature of the dark. Crustaceous, I scuttled across turgid seas of traffic. I was necessary but somehow loathesome.

Columnists, niteclub comics, YMHA intellectuals and gimlet-eyed cloakandsuiters found my accent laughable, my temper vile, my thought-processes stale and vicious. To them I was the lowest common denominator of Mob Man. Members of groups that thirsted for vengeance on account of wrongs fancied or real, spewed their venom(y) on me. I was the butt of every tinhorn jerk or hood with the price of a ride.

Tall tales are told of my multifarious sins. I roll lushes, it is said, insulted old ladies, clipped Live Ones, and delighted in taking Outoftowners for a ride around the Mulberry Bush. I even bragged of such misdeeds to others of the Gang, at a table in the Automat or whiling away the time on a hackstand, just to prove what a rollicking ass I could be. I am a stereotype of vulgarity, a loudmouth. And I recited my lines exactly as they were given to me, without changing a comma. The only crime I was innocent of was that of bitterness. I was much too dumb, they said, for that.

Yet there was something in me hidden away, unknown. Something that stirred when clean winds blew out of distant spaces. Though vanished from the eye of love, from even the memory of friends, that something writhed in agonies I could not even know were spiritual. Indeed, buried inside the armorplate of my swampdwelling species, what could I know of either spirit or sense? All I knew was a dull loathing for work that exhausted and shocked, but left no pause in which to lean, and loaf, and invite the soul. I was an appendage of the machine. I had no soul.

Unceasingly, for seven years, I made the circuit of neon and stone: Times Square to Chinatown, Park Avenue to Forest Hills, the Penn to Grand Central, Coney Island to Delancey Street. Of that arctic vast without, I knew nothing.

In time, I came to think that I would never wake to human speech again. Middleaged, I would probably drop dead at the wheel while rolling along a superhighway under the naked moon. I would be smashed up and conveniently cremated in the wreck. In the world I inhabited, my silence was bitter as the stink of a dead cigar, black as the frozen, twisted tubes of a Broadway "spectacular" gone dead in a storm. Until the last lousy lush is tucked away in his tasselated sty in Riverdale or Beekman Place, I swore, I shall keep that silence unbroken. Never shall I utter a word in praise or blame. Never shall I reveal the flatulent secrets of this grimy trade.

THE HACKIE RIDES A GHOST

Take a look, a good look, at the guy in the cap, sitting under a picture of himself, the bruised features blurred in the plastic, illumined through the night with number and name. "In case of complaint," the license reads, "report this man to Police Department." A criminal? Psycho? No, only a Hackie. Compelled to wear a cap, to be subservient; "in case of complaint" his testimony nothing worth; domineered by passenger, boss, police . . . the guy ticketed, labelled, libelled: "Hackie." There, but for the grace of God and economic circumstance goes who—whom—him—ME?

Yeah, it could happen. Even to you. Picture yourself in this guy's boots. Out of a job, nowhere to turn. Can you drive a car? Take out a hack license, Mac! Did you know, could you know what you were letting yourself in for? Instead of warning you, briefing you on the dangers, taking you into custody for your own protection, committing you to Bellevue or Mattewan to think it over while watching the antics of hackie-inmates, they welcomed and waved you into the stockade, gave you the old shape-up treatment, primed you for the slaughter.

You said to yourself, or being foolish, to others: "I'll stay in this racket a month or two, make a buck, have a look around, get a job in my old line or take that connection I've been waiting for."

Yeh, yeh; just going along for the ride. Point is, you're travelling on a circular roadbed, the express stops at no stations and your ticket reads "Nowhere." What time is it—yesterday? Gosh, you forgot to answer that letter from the bank, inviting you to take over their Wall Street branch. Well, there'll be another one along any minute. Meantime, relax in front of the Waldorf: 2 hours from now you'll be Headout, a jerk will hop in, muzzling his girl. Take us to the Plahza, plee-uz. Forty cents on the clock. He slips you a half and runs like a teef.

And looka what happened during that forty cent journey. While the cheapjack and his jill consummated their champagne romance, you had a near-collision, running your blood pressure up again, got into a hassle with an

outoftown driver, got a lecture from a cop for almost passing a light, and finally dropped the cargo but got caught in a minor traffic jam, thus killing another 15-20 minutes. Or do I exaggerate?

So grit your teeth, kid, while grinding gears: it's all music, and it listens good. Couple of sour notes in a symphony of how many millions means nothing at all in this scheme of things. "I could be bounded in a nutshell, yet count myself King of infinite space." Do you dream, kid? You're an old man now but you wear that cap, I keep thinking of you as just a green youth. Hear them call you "Boy," "Cabbie," "Mac"? Will you never grow up? You played 1-2-3 but the number came out 3-2-1? Whatever became of that old gal of yours? Sometimes, cruising along a deserted street at night with a high wind blowing up puffs of steam from hot sewers and only the slap and rattle of loose fender to keep you company, you wonder what happened to her, and to that life of yours, to that deathless soul they tell about in a hush at church to the sound of organs—

Hey you, guy in the cap! do you dream dreams?

When it rains, rains on the black, black stone, and the houses lean and melt together, do you hear the spatter the sputter of rain in your heart?

Are you dead, Mac? Stone-cold dead in the marketplace? But no, not quite: I hear you chatter:

"He's a ex-jockey hisself an he gizz me a tip on dis horse" . . .

Still going along for the ride, I see. The comeback is easy on a circular track. But the train never stops, and it's yesterday before you know it. Sometimes I hear you talk to yourself:

"Never gonna wear a cap no more. Never gonna take no guff, no crap. I'm troo, troo wid all dat stuff . . ."

Put yourself in the other guy's boots. Out of a job, nowhere to turn. Yeah, it could happen. Even to YOU.

DREAMS, SUBWAYS, NIGHT THOUGHTS

I am dreaming at the wheel while the cab is parked at a hackstand, its motor thrumming, windshield wipers slapping at the black wet world outside. Let it rain. Let people scrabble for cabs outside Grand Central and Penn Stations, and curse all derelict cabbies who sit unprofitably at a curb and dream, and wait for no passengers. A passenger now would disturb the even flow of thought. (*or*, the even flow of my reflections, break the spell of memory.) I reach back, lock the doors, and turn the light switch off. But I let the motor run, just for company . . .

I dream that I am a child again in the Bronx. I am in the kitchen of our railroad flat. It is evening. I have much homework still to do. My cheeks are flushed with the swift play and tumult of the street. I can hear my big brother Benny, ten years older than . . .

*   *   *

There are delicate tints in the sky when I emerge from the subway in the late afternoon. This is my weary morning and I am less brisk about it than the workaday, day-working fold who can quit with the broiling   and hasten past me   to beat the rush. They do not know what a precious thing this daylight is. How can they know? But how quickly it fades for me!

*   *   *

. . . the evening was transformed. The moon grew golden, the streets were purple and smoky (dusky?). The lights had a musky smell. This was release from the straitlaced, mean, pinchpenny . . .

*   *   *

The old-fashioned train (riding?) carriage was a roomy affair. If a man were tired and inclined to sleep, he could rest an elbow on a conveniently low ledge, stretch his legs, and doze off. He had room in which to breathe, an atmosphere of passable human warmth surrounding him, and no heartsqueez-

ing grip of time to destroy his disposition and health. Today, even the design of subway cars shows the distance we have gone towards inhumanity and discomfort.

*   *   *

The train came in on the wrong side of the platform. It was labelled correctly, but who reads labels? One steps off the express side of the platform and one expects to enter an express train; after a while, one looks out to watch station signs. Travel became a reflex. So the man, a   and weary night worker spending perhaps his last few grains of energy, stepped inside the car and sat down heavily. He was tired, and lately had been feeling twinges around the heart. Medical bills yet? He couldn't afford it; wouldn't even be able to take the time off for checkups, treatments. But lately, he'd been tossing about all day, too exhausted to get proper sleep, and only snoozed off toward the last hour. Then he'd jump up in shock at the alarm clock's ringing, turn it off, and rush about the house, washing up, shaving, getting his own breakfast, cleaning up afterwards. His wife had taken a job to help make ends meet. He saw her but rarely. Ah, now perhaps he could catch a snooze. Careful, though—don't mess up by passing the 57th Street Station.

Those trained reflexes woke him in plenty of time. He looked out; the train was passing 49th Street. He sighed; stamped his left foot, that had been crossed over the right and was dead to the world. Bad circulation. He stood up and moved to the door on the left. Well, here we go! He hitched up his pants. But, strangely, the train was passing on a center rail and he saw the station move across him through a blur of black posts as the train picked up speed. It is not going to stop, he thought. I'll be late and lose the job.

*   *   *

Eating late just before dropping off, in exhaustion, to the overpowering demands of sleep, makes for pressure on the belly, which in turn gives bad dreams. You never remember the worst of them. The thousand little shocks experienced during the working night are relived, reinterpreted, and embellished by subconscious terrors and fantasy. A macabre one I can remember . . .

*   *   *

I am crossing a great bridge in blinding rain and wind. The cab under me coughs and grunts like a wild, emetic beast; the wheel wobbles in my hand. I am giving her all the gas I can. "Her?" Is it the cab itself that drives me, rather than the other way 'round? Surely I sense an evil personality in this flying machine. A will to self-destruction whose real target is *me*. Making me careless of speed limits and signal lights.

*   *   *

149

endpiece for a/intro: *NIGHT AND THE HACKIE*
   or b/l'envoi: *HACKIE RIDES A GHOST*

The subway ride home, in the still gray night before the dawn, is the payoff. Ghosts nudge the elbow of the dozing, weary pedalpusher. He wants to sleep, to forget. Gaunt figures leer in his dreams, and crowd him awake. He looks about him in the train, blear-eyed and miserable. Far down the train is another Hackie, slouching at a window seat with nothing to stare at outside but blackness. The dream-haunted one addresses him in a bellow:

"The cab broke down again on me tonight and I lost two hours waiting for the tow-truck. When they pulled it into the garage, the mechanic showed me how the wheel was ready to come off at a touch. Just a touch! No bolts to hold it. Lucky I wasn't killed. I coulda been killed, the damn thing was wobbling all over the road . . ."

He shakes his head; it's too much for one man to understand. How they could send a driver out in a lump like that . . . Down at the other end, his buddie grunts some reply, and is silent. The man who has spoken woos sleep once more. Chewing his wad of gum slowly and deliberately, he shakes his head from side to side. No, he seems to be saying, I can't believe it, this isn't happening to me at all. His eyes are closed; inside, great wounds gape open.

The train jogs on and on through the tunnelled night that has no end and no beginning. Slowly, almost imperceptibly, the flatlands of Brooklyn appear, and the Cabbie snaps into wakefulness. He speaks in an even, wondering tone. "An hour and a half coming in. An hour and a half going back. That's three hours wasted. Then an hour on the shape-up, at least. That makes four. Now I lose two more hours stranded on the road. That's six hours without a penny. Six hours!" The thought of this waste, this loss, hits him like a slug in the belly. He looks dazed. Then he sighs heavily . . . "It's a long, tiresome ride," he says, addressing noone in particular.

The other Cabbie wearily pulls himself to his feet as the train nears his station. He gazes about, as if searching for something, some word of strength and counsel. His eyes stop at a train poster. He reads:

> THE PERSON OPPOSITE YOU
> would be wise to get a
> box of XYZ cough drops at
> the next stop. Excellent
> for coughs that result
> from colds . . .

Oh, no, he thinks, that person isn't suffering from any cough that comes from a cold, or even from a cold that comes from a cough. He's a Hackie, a Zombie like me. All he needs, and he needs it bad, is the coffin they carry you off in . . .

150

AFTER-HOURS SUBWAY CLUB

3 A. M. That's when the nuts come out on the street, said the young cop. And not only on the street. It's bags and bundles time on the subway; it's rags and scuffle time. The shuffling, disheartened trains—smell of grease, vomit, disinfectant, banana skins. In corners by black windows, in compartments behind partitions, sit creatures in the foul stink of their diseases; dishevelled, glum, vacuous.

*   *   *

. . . cruised thru the lox-and-bagel sector, Avenue A to D, at 3 A. M. The houses seemed to lean over in that weary, companionable way peculiar to the

East Side and to no other neighborhood. Perhaps because here generations of immigrants had lived en masse, surging and hopeful . . .

*   *   *

I have passed through streets late at night, deserted, empty, silent. And in the unblinking light of high lamps I have sensed the sadness and agony of solitary souls. They wander about and are lost. The vagrants, the poets, the whores, the psychos, failures, the killers—all the demented and despairing folk who are cast off by the whirling gears of the city, washed up like scum on the black sidewalks by the tides of time.

Many times I saw Max Bodenheim, the poet ruined by alcohol, striding hatless in the cold, with a strange glitter in his stary (stony?) eye, an envelope of poems under his arm, muttering through clenched teeth. And at 3 A. M. on an eastside street, just weeks before his horrible death, I saw the youth who murdered him walk by—a dark, sullen youth fondling a cat inside his sweater —recognized him as such by his picture in the paper. My cab was parked at the curb when this obvious psychopath came by. The cop standing nearby winked to me and said: "All the nuts are out at 3 A. M."

*   *   *

Incurables are the only kind of crazy people worth meeting. Only when the entire psychiatric profession has given them up as hopeless can these fortunate ones relax, and be their own delightfully zany zany selves. No more worries about adapting to a world loony beyond their wildest fancies: they can jabber away till the end of time, make noises, tapdance, gesticulate without fear of snoopers and lubricitous peepers taking notes and solemnly nodding their heads.

HACKING FRAGMENTS

For *Chapter 10*
The night of the Hackie is deep, dark, and beyond all known stars. How many howls in the night I have heard! How many lost souls, drifting along the pavement like wisps of steam from gratings, have I passed and noted! A sullen-eyed youth slinks beneath a corner streetlamp. It is cold, bitter but he wears no jacket. Inside his shirt he cuddles a squirming cat. The cop on the beat winks to me. "All the nuts come out at 3 A. M.," he says. Months later, the youth's picture is flashed on page 1 of the tabloids. He has murdered the Village poet, Bodenheim, shot him and plunged a knife into the back of his wife. A cat-lover, a maniac destroyer. Another face in the night . . .

The city is full of dead poets at night, most of whom live out their poems
in lonesome walks because they are too scared or too tired to write them. The
city bludgeons them by day: they are truckdrivers, ad writers, gadget salesmen.
I knew one who hemstitched matzos in a dingy east side factory. But at night
the snakes of thought uncoil; sliding out between the prison bars, they emerge
upon the sparkling pavement and slither away, free at last. These may be
poisoners or harmless, depending on the species. I have seen both from the
vantage point of my cab.

Bodenheim, the poet with staring eyes, the bohemian drunkard, I had
seen many times before on the streets. Joe Gould, that wispy-bearded word-
wastrel who would be a prophet, groaning as though his heart would break as
he crossed behind my cab on Seventh Avenue. One   . Where are
your jests now, Joe, I wondered. Nothing so sad as a neglected clown. And
the peephole columnist whose quick puns and jazzed-up slogans are feared

and revered along the rialto, walking, alone, on the unglamorous pavement at 3 A. M.; he is no more than any other sourpuss cloak and suiter in a bad season. How much money is needed to give a man ease? A cold wind blows through the streets of the city, and the wolf must howl. Pauper or millionaire, it is all one to the malevolent wind. Man is naked, and yearns for the approval of his kind.

Roche the psychopathetic killer—cut the throat of a grayhaired Polish cabbie just outside the 22nd Street police station. Another babyfaced punk, . . .

(Either for a dissertation on The Hound, or for an introduction to Chapter 11: "Hackie Tintypes," or for Chapter 13: "Call Me Porkchop.")

Hackies don't stick together; it only looks that way in heavy traffic. They are, in fact, the most vituperatively self-hating group of men in existence. They hate one another's guts, and with reason. (or, Among New York's ten thousand hackies, there is little joi de vivre, no esprit de corps, and only a limited kind of savoir faire. They are a glum bunch who hate each other's guts.) But of sangfroid and chutzpah they have mucho. Full of bluster and bluff, the socalled "average hackie" will commit himself to any dogmatic

Hackie– "individual"

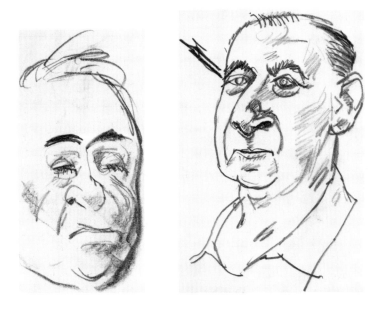

opinion that is not at variance with his favorite newspaper's editorial page. He will tell you who ought to be shot, drawn and quartered, and who deserves a Congressional Medal for having stolen a million bucks. And he will tell it in impeccably dull and dirty lingo. There he is right in the swim of the merde moderne. I have heard actors, actresses, politicians, Park Avenue dowagers, and other monied whores sound off, and they do no better with Shakespeare's language. Only, the cabbie sounds more natural.

When the tag, "rugged individualist," is pinned to the diaper of that cruelly abandoned and motherless waif, the New York Hackie, I permit myself a chuckle in between sobs. Hoo, hoo, hoo! Because he snarls up and at traffic, because he has to scramble the streets for pay dirt, because he spits opinions like oysters with every catarrhal breath he draws, the cabbie becomes, in the sentimentalist view, a real person behind the wheel. Alas, this is simply not true. The only time the cabbie becomes real, even to himself, is when he is miles removed from the working milieu—at home, on his day off. But on the job, he is a zero, a smudged and grimy rubberstamp, okaying the obvious. His reflexes are routine, unhealthy, and predictable. He is just a sad sack with more wrinkles than most.

Removed from the seat of privilege behind the wheel, your routine hackie is the dullest conversationalist this side of Hell. With no captive audience to mumble appreciation at his smart-sounding cliches and swiftly lethal judgements, he is revealed as an oaf with no thought higher than the pork-and-beans of his daily earnings. When his dismal rounds are done, he will foregather in the home garage or coffeepot for the sole purpose of toting

155

up, to a penny, what he earned that night. "I got 27 calls, I was out to LaGuardia twice, I caught one back to 72nd, I done 3   jobs." There are no faces in all this talk. There is no flavor of a street; the city is a shapeless mass and life is a traffic switchboard where amorphous metal objects move on green, stop on red, and go on endlessly, without purpose, from the cradle (garage) to the grave (junkheap).

Hackies are just as individual as unsugared Automat doughtnuts, and they exhibit all the rugged qualities of a male spider about to be lured, screwed and devoured. I mean, why do you suppose these guys have developed no effective organization to protect their rights or boost their earnings in all these years of labor struggles and victories? Why do they permit themselves to be bulldozed, badgered, pre-judged and slapped around (for tiny infractions of a thousand senseless rules) by the Hack Bureau? Why is it they can be bounced out of a 20-year job for a traffic accident which they did not cause? All this, because they are *rugged*? Tell that to your Aunt Tallahassee.

Because of the brash words and antics of your Average Hackie, a moron to the wheel form, every man (or woman—there are a few) who fills out a tripcard in New York has been labelled a loudmouth, a braggart, a bold thief. Believe me, 'tis not so. True, you cannot remain meek and humble on this job, even if you were born that way and psychiatrists looked on you with   . You have to get tough at times, or lose all human values.

(For introduction to Chapter 11: "Hackie Tintypes," or for Chapter 13: "Call Me Porkchop," or to be entitled "A Night Man's Daymares.")

What depths of bitterness and venom in the hackie's lacerated soul! Remember the night, Benny, you were shocked to hear a cocky, frowzy little old hackie, who should at least have respected his own gray fuzz, curse you out with expletives among which "rat-bastard" was the least vile? You could have pushed his ugly phiz through the window of his cab, but you were too startled even to answer. So this was your fellow-worker, your colleague, your contemporary, your class brother? You wondered what experience of life could make for such an accumulation of villainy and filth. A mere brush in traffic had exposed the gangrenous heart and malfunctioning brain, and you were seared by the sight. Well, it's been five years in the hellhole, boy, five years of nightmare, and now you know. Sitting behind the wheel like a victim stretched on the rack, snarled at and spat upon, commanded and cursed, reprimanded and threatened and "dimed to death." What have you learned, Benny? Let's go over the lesson . . .

(or)

I remember the day I was shocked to hear a cocky, frowzy, little hackie who should have respected his own gray fuzz, curse me out with vile expressions, among which "rat-bastard" was the least rancid. I wondered what experience of life could make for such bitterness, such villainous coarseness, such hate. Well, I've hacked in this hellhole for five nightmare years and now I know. Now I too, pricked and slapped by the hardwhore city, spit upon and snarled at by cop, hack-inspector, despatcher,   , as well as every snob or drunk of a passenger—I too on occasion yelp and snarl and spit, whirl a wheel, grind a gear . . .

Despite the loudmouth brag, the wiseguy snarl, the greasy whine, what remains basic about the character of the hound Hackie is his treachery and cowardice. Stopped at a red light, he will open a bout of sympathetic small talk with another hackie, for the sole purpose of distracting his attention, for just as soon as the light flicks off, he will dash across the other guy's bumper to pick up a waiting fare he has glimpsed out of the tail of his eye. To the manager, he will try to stick needles in the other guy by tall tales of big tips, windfalls, etc. He'll rat on anybody who talks union or liberal while mouthing pious cliches of the hour.

Some of the Hounds get so low, they could crawl under a snake's belly and never so much as tickle him. In the wintertime, this type of Hound carries a bottle or can up front with him to urinate in, so he won't lose time off the job. But accidents will happen . . .

One bitter cold afteroon, after having waited 1½ hours on the shapeup, Itch the Despicable sent me out on a banged-up old load. "It's a steady man's cab," he said. "Go to work." I pulled out of the garage in a hurry, anxious to make up for some of the time wasted. It was a very cold day, and perhaps that was why it took some minutes before I got a whiff of something peculiar. An odor, like that of a dead rat in a tenement wall . . . I was out in traffic already, and nothing I could do about it. I got a hail. The man got in, gave me the address, and leaned back. Then he leaned forward, and sniffed. I felt self-conscious, but didn't say a word. He sniffed again. Finally, "You been hacking the Fulton Fish Market?" he demanded to know. "I just started to work, Mister," I told him truthfully. "I don't know from nothing." "You got a nose, ain't you?" he snapped. "Yeah," I replied. "Could be the day man who belongs to this cab likes stale herring. Or maybe he rode a spoiled passenger." "Well, I'm getting out here," decided my fare. And he paid me off, and walked.

Every race and religion has its imbeciles, its hoodlums, its sado-masochists. Among the Jews, the sure sign of the envenomed self-torturer is the facile way he has of employing Yiddish phrases and epithets to indicate his scorn of you and all the inferior world.

When it's compulsory to wear a cap on the job, and have a warning picture and number stuck up in view of all, life takes on a different aspect, and you know what it means to be looking out at the world through invisible bars. The cap is your official uniform; soon the dust and fumes in the street give you the correct hackie pallor; the only difference remaining between you and a convict is that he, at least, does not have to scramble for each meal with claw and fang.

Among the hackies themselves there is tacit awareness of their status, and they joke at those who would seek to conceal it, or act "different." Anybody who carries a book or The New York Times instead of the usual "set" of tabloids is called "Professor." A man who likes to smoke a good cigar and wear a white shirt, is known as "Senator" or "Governor." Also, there is the pecking order. The guy who glues himself to the wheel 14 hours a night and brings in "big bookings" becomes a "Hound" or a "Groessa Fadeena" (Big Earner) depending on how you evaluate him personally. Nobody loves a "hungry" Hackie—he'll swerve in front of you and stop on a dime to steal a call. On the other hand, if he reports in to the garage with less than the average bookings for the night, he's a "porkchop," harmless but pitiable.

But no matter what the hackie does, nobody loves him. The boss despises him and will give him the bounce in favor of a younger and more energetic driver; his fellow cabbies look upon him as a tricky competitor; his passengers mistrust him; the cops look at him as guilty of anything. In the course of the jungle wars, the "nice guy" gets chewed up and outmanoeuvered. A "hound" shoos him off for a fare, blows a whistle behind him and then outraces him, gabs him into falling behind . . . And they encourage dissensions, put a premium on dishonesty and gangster tactics. How? By ignoring the taxiline and grabbing a cruiser who just rolled up; by crankiness and shirt-tapping (who'll bother to return a lost umbrella to a skunk?); by sneering and high-hatting, trying to deprive a decent-spoken cabbie of his human dignity and worth. How often have I writhed . . .

Hackies suffer from occupational loneliness and often wind up as blabber-mouths, exhibiting a weak, drooling volubility to passengers in which sense and nonsense are inextricably mixed. Among themselves in coffeepots, on hacklines, they become braggarts, washerwomen, or rowdies.

What makes some Hackies so conceited? Well, they have their name right up there in lights, you know. Also their picture, large as life but not so noisy. And their number is up, too. (The day I took out a hack license, my number was up.) Most hackies play their license numbers. That way, they figure they'll count for something. Just when the number is due to hit, according to the law of averages—once a cabbie called it the "numeratical law"—the year is up, they have to renew their hack license and they're off on a new number. Also, they acquire a fund of knowledge, not from books—from bookies.

Cabbies are popularly supposed to know *everything*. A passenger gets in the cab. "Will it rain, driver?" He thinks just because the Hackie is sitting next to a meter, that makes him a meter-ologist. Not true at all. Of course, a real gabby cabbie can lacerate you with sharp, jagged points of misinformation. He'll tell you hack stories dating back to when he drove a covered wagon and used a sundial instead of a clock. When you get out at your destination, he's sorry because you interrupted his flow of gab. But don't think it's all for free. "Hey, Mr., I told you 13 anecdotes and you only gimme a dime. You owe me 3 cents." He bends your ear, then he throws you out on it.

But it's the Hungry Joe . . .

Why do so many hackies act punchy? There are reasons.

Each hoodlum, each sadistic punk he encounters leaves a mark on the hackie's mind and soul. Often, he will mistakenly sympathize with the expressed ires of a drunk or a psycho, only to have this whiner's loathsome humanity-hating personality shoved in his face.

Remember this: people are poison. Rats in your own garage, who will steal a job on the sheet or squeal a complaint on the sly. Neurotics and bums and stiffshirt, inhuman customers to tip you cheap and treat you hard; watch them and beware. Beware the dime-tipper, the skunk, the neurotic, the deadbeat. Beware of Bronxite, Harlemite, Jersey Jerk, Parkevvener. Beware of Shantyowners, outoftowners, countryclubbers, couponclippers,   , congenital muggers. Whether they belong to a Majority or a Minority, a big church or a little one, a right-or left-wing, it makes no difference. Truck-driver, careerwoman, TV pimp, intellectual, social worker, executive, sailor, storeclerk, bum—they're just naturally cheap, inconsiderate, selfish, mean. They think that a seat back there makes them . . .

CABBIE SILHOUETTES

"THE SHERIFF"

"The Sheriff" was a little rollypolly oldster who always had a smile and a cheery "Hello, Lad," for the boys in the garage. He was built so close to the ground that, when he drove his cab, it looked like automation had come at last to the taxi industry. Off the cab, he looked like a Disney dwarf who had stepped into a deep mudhole. The long topcoats he persisted in wearing, even into the spring, increased the effect. He had the best manners of anyone in the garage, and was never ruffled by anything.

The nickname originally was "The Seraph." He was given the name for what was his fanatical aversion to all forms of swearing. Not only were the words for all vegetative and sexual functions taboo in his presence, but also the mildest damning or jocular allusions to women. He referred to his revered wife always as "my lady." His many sons, of whose gargantuan physiques and insatiable appetites for food he spoke with awe, were all "fine lads." The sheriff had one daughter, and that daughter had a boy, making his grandaddy proud enough to burst. When the grandson had a "briss," the Sheriff came into the garage loaded with cigarboxes, five bottles of good whiskey, and Momma's best Jewish sponge cake. Never was so little shorn skin celebrated with so many skinfuls.

MONTE, OR STORY OF A HOMICIDE

Monte talked like his fists were always ready to swing. A stubby little guy with lots of hair yet and a build like Tony Galento's, it looked like he might really back up his words if necessity arose, as maybe it would. Because a scrappy hackie can get into dozens of hassles each night on the street if he wants to, or if he likes to stare and curse, or kick up a fuss. Plenty of blustering eyes are looking to get a fat lip in traffic. Not to mention run-ins with customers, which can also easily reach the punching stage.

But a man had also to think about his bread and butter, and no married middle-aged man like Monte can afford to lose his license, or even have it suspended for any length of time. You don't make too much dough on this job, but where can you find another? The men didn't take Monte's gab too seriously. They'd seen too many like him who ran away from a fight. They had problems of their own.

Monte was considered a new man in the garage, even though he'd been on the job four months. He told Slimey he wanted a steady cab; he was sick of shaping-up. After all, he worked six nights and brought in more than the average "bookings." But Slimey didn't like his tone of voice, and since no bills changed hands under the table, he turned him down. Monte knew what the score was but he'd be damned if he paid any kickbacks, he said. He just stood out there on the shape-up line and tried to stare Slimey down. But Slimey ignored him. Up there on his podium pimply little Slimey was the biggest guy in the joint. But he never openly insulted Monte, like he would do with impunity to Schmendrick. Monte might not just quit and say stick the job you know where. He'd swing once, and Slimey would be collecting hospital expenses. Or pushing up daisies, like one of the Bosses who treated the wrong guy to the rough side of his tongue. That concrete floor was hard.

Jakey Pox had it in for Monte and everyone in the garage knew it. He would keep him standing there in the shape-up until Monte was ready to bust, then he might toss him a tripsheet like throwing a nickel to a beggar, or he'd just hand him his little payroll card and say, "No more cabs. Take the day off." Nobody knew why Monte continued to stick it out at this garage when he could go anywhere else and get a steady car, and go out earlier.

JOE PICCOLO

Crazier than Joe Piccolo it is hard to get. What can you say of a man who, with a gun pressed to the back of his skull, turns to face the holdup man, remarking: "I sure wish I had your racket, buddie"? Of course, after a few more unfeeling comments on that order, the robber stashed his gat and walked off in a huff. Lunatics, he probably reflected, are the wrong people to do business with.

It's not that Joe is naturally cruel or anything. He is well aware of the exigencies prevailing in the stick-up trade, as well as in panhandling, selling, pimping, manufacturing, and many another field of endeavor. He would like to help everybody out really, but what can one man do? Joe's way of beating the hidden persuader is a simple one. He plays nuts.

In appearance, Joe is a dead ringer for that other great and eccentric artist, Picasso. White-haired, solidly built, his potato face is sturdy and quizzical, like a Breton peasant's. He has been hacking over 30 years, but it hasn't made him brassy or foulmouthed, like so many others. When he speaks, which is not very often . . .

He was the wittiest cabbie in the city—and for the smallest tips. He'd squeeze a gang of six into the cab, and when he asked where to, and somebody answered "Luchow's," meaning the restaurant, he'd come back fast with "Gezundheit!" which naturally broke everybody up. When they got there, some chuckling fellow would slip him a Big Dime and he'd have to swallow fast in order to keep from rattling out some remark which would have spoiled everything and made bad friends. So he acquired an ulcer or two which he couldn't afford to have X-rayed or treated, and who knows, maybe he developed something psychologically, because on not a few occasions he caught himself mumbling words full of bile and venom. Such a situation, you would guess, cannot long endure in this happy land of freedom. And you'd be right, brother—dead right.

CALIGARI

Caligari, the day despatcher, lives in a world of perpetual night. I have never known this mean, scowling yerkel to have a good word for anyone. I used to chuck him a pack of cigarettes in return for the "privilege" of taking a cab home Sunday mornings. Then his rasping, foul tongue got under my skin, and I decided to forego the pleasure. He takes kickbacks and grafts from the day men but continually complains that the Weasel is making out much better. Hints that he could tell things if he wished that would make Big Mokus hit the ceiling. Since he keeps running to the boss with tales and insinuations about the cabbies' sins all the time, it's likely this is sour-grape stuff, or else he's involved in the doings himself, or he'd have spilled it up in the office long ago. A perfect rodent.

The Farmer came in with an accident last week, and Big Mokus fired him. Didn't matter that he was standing still when the other car smacked him. Didn't matter that he worked for the outfit eleven years, and had only six minor accidents. Driving through heavy city traffic six nights a week all that time. Big Mokus is a heavy contributor to the local synagogue and all religious causes. But any pretext is good enough to shove out an old-timer, slowed down by years of taking gaff, and replace him with fresh blood. Also saves on that vacation bonus. And never one hour of severance pay given.

Schmaltz rooms in the same building with Caligari. He claims the guy is human. But I doubt it. "Did you ever see him smile?" I ask. But Schmaltz explains, he got things on his mind. Like what? Debts. A delinquent son who's in and out of jail. Yes, granted we all have our troubles, but is that enough of a reason to turn rat? The other day a fed-up cabbie sounded off about big Mokus, the Boss, just mouthstuff, but it got back to the office and the man got fired. Who done it? Caligari. "That's life," shrugs Schmaltz, who works for another garage now and feels somewhat remote. Bending an

elbow at the bar with Caligari, who had just won 480 smackers on a number, when the guy, still unsmiling, confessed: "I'm a Boss's man." Now *everybody* knows it.

ABIE

Abie Weitzkorn had a lumpy face. A guy pushing 40 looking like if you took a cheap, gray, stitched-canvas bag, about the size of a soccer ball, filled it with wet cement, swung it from the rafters and got a heavyweight puncher with taped knucks to jab at it in several unlikely places; then, stuck two glass immies in it for eyes, drew a straight line for a mouth, let the whole thing set, you'd have the main planes, the lights and shadows, the glimmer and brood of Abie Weitzkorn, night hackie. But screw in a weak yellow bulb over his head for a cab-light and surround him with darkness, for that's the milieu and the clue to understanding, if you want a real natural history exhibit.

But Abie wasn't half as tough as he looked. Because he looked bad-tough, and he wasn't that. And while he was bone-hard and bitter enough, those glass immies had a laugh in them while they were sizing you up. But the straight mouth said nothing. Abie was not the typical, gabby cod who likes to ramble on with the passengers because he's nervous, or lonely, or wants to butter them up for a good tip. He stuck his mitt out and took what was given, returning a courteous but colorless "thanks," because the stinking job didn't mean you had to grovel. But inside, while he was driving or waiting or writing up the tripsheet, Abie was laughing at himself and the world.

(Editors' Note: Spector penned on his typescript the alternate name of Sam or Silent Sam for Abie, who seems to be a portrayal of his brother-in-law.)

FAKOKTA LANDLORD

(Editors' Note: Spector's Cabbie Silhouettes included three versions—"Fakokta Landlord," "F. Fakokta Landlord" and "The 'Pishka' "—all of which are included here for comparative purposes.)

This fleabitten, mangy oldtimer who has no smile and no spark of curiosity is known by many pseudonyms indicative of his nature and possessions. Fakokta Landlord, Wooden Indian, Ahza Putz, are a few of them. Unmellowed by the years of subhuman moiling in the dark, he is cynical and irreverent of all things but strangely obsequious in the presence of the fleet Boss, who despises him and will fire him, regardless of years of service, on the first pretext, for that is the standard fleet practice. As machines and men wear out, the former are repaired, the latter thrown out. But Chowderhead can't face this fact. He imagines himself a buddy-buddy of the Boss, who was once a despised Hackie himself.

The fleet Boss is a caricature of a mobster. A foul-mouthed gorilla, unlettered and unimaginative even in his use of obscenities, his language is matched by his jungle ethics and zoo manners. Esconced behind his desk, he spits oysters on the floor, breaks wind, belches, picks studiously at his nose and teeth, and roars invective and insult to be heard all over the office. It matters to him not at all that his acts are witnessed, not only by male subordinates, some of whom are his despised and lowly relatives, but by stenos and office girls of the same age as his daughter, whom he is sending to private schools for the acquisition of "culture."

F. FAKOKTA LANDLORD

He is gimlet-eyed, hatchet-faced, gaunt. Three rattrap tenements he owns, other parcels here and there, but he dresses like a Boweryite and hacks six nights a week—a hungry hound. Only a few hackies know the secret of his wealth; the others sniff something rotten in his personality and shy off at his approach. Not that he seeks human companionship; far from it. He is content to come and go like a shadow, keeping his parched lips shut and his thoughts to himself. Only on the payoff line, when the long night is done and the men are horsing around, does the itch come to make contact with some mean dig or stale gag stolen from the garbage can and hoarded over the years.

164

"Hey, Ahza! Ahza Putz . . . That all ya booked, three pounds? What was ya doing, pullin' off? . . . Hey, Saniflush! 'Ja kok today?" . . . His stubbled jaw creaks open in a weak simper, revealing a few yellow fangs.

Although the tabloid readers, numbers players and belly thinkers whom he addresses are prone to no more elegant speech themselves, they find in his raspy whine no humor, no hint of friendliness, and never even bother to grin a response. But the Wooden Indian, as he has been nicknamed, feels no pain. He's had his moment, and he's satisfied. He is happiest when someone on the line turns up with a smackup to report, a traffic ticket, or some other trouble. Then a gloat comes into his voice. "Looka the shape of this one!" he croaks.

After turning in his bookings, the Fakokta Landlord starts the long trudge to the subway. Alone, he hunches his narrow shoulders, keeps his hands in his pockets and peers about like a beaked scavenger. As he walks he keeps fingering the coins in his pocket, adding them up, estimating tips, expenditures, gross and net income. He can tell a hack from a handsaw, a dime from a penny, and he isn't crazy enough to pay 15 cents for "coffee without" at the all-night cafeteria on top of the hill, though it is a drear cold morning and a cup of java would just hit the spot. No, he is no sucker, and he needs no luxuries. Everything that can possibly be saved, he saves. He even prefers to go without certain strategic teeth than give his money to a dentist for replacement. When a green young hackie asks him how to make out a trip-sheet or what's a good spot to hack, he replies, "Does Macy's tell Gimbel's?", and turns away. Nobody ever got something for nothing from him.

Yet I have heard there is no smoother finagler on the street when it comes to tips, overcharges and other angles. His beat is midtown, he wiggles easily out of taking passengers to Brooklyn or the Bronx, . . .

165

The cashier's a snarler, a mean, hardbitten cod who stands inside his steel cage and spits sarcasm as the men line up to turn in their night's "bookings." Tired and worn from pushing, battling traffic, taking guff from the passengers, and now they must face this barking. His job is a routine checking of figures and cash, yet he has turned it into one involving favoritism and the wielding of power, all through the gawky meekness of these exploited fools. He'll make acid comments on their trustworthiness and capacity to work, imply that they're lying down on the job, utter veiled threats or indulge himself in cheap buffoonery at the expense of the blinking yerkel before him: "Some shape you're in! Dy'ya know Ahza . . . Ahza Schmoe!" And all the time, if they're not alert, and how can they be at four and five in the morning, he'll rob them blind. "Hey, you, you're a dollar short. Come across!" Having surreptitiously removed a bill from the pile, he'll pass it back through the bars. "Count it again!"

Comes Friday, he'll stick a beer mug outside the cage with a crudely lettered sign reading: "Thank You Cashier." This is the pishka, or collection cup, into which coins are clinked by these gutless cabbies as they shuffle up to turn in the receipts and mumble their insincere respects. Nobody actually respects Jakey Gloober, this squat, illfavored toad who cheats and scorns the men and then runs to the Boss to snitch on them. "Rat," "Whore," "Boss's Man," is the way they refer to him privately. But it's "Hiya, Jakey, have a cigar" to his face. They know that he has more money than God, that he owns 3 or 4 rattrap tenements on the East Side, yet the quarters and halves are chipped into the kitty "irregardless."

GARAGE

The oldtimers, drivers of "steady" cabs, slip in and out of the piss-stinking garage like shadows, like gray lizards. Tightlipped little guys, with bitterness and venom lurking in the depths of their lacerated souls. A green hackie asks one of them a simple question, how to figure the "readings" on a trip-sheet. "Does Macy's tell Gimbel's?" he snarls and turns away disgustedly. This is an oldtimer they call the *Fakokta Landlord*. A gimlet-eyed, hatchet-faced specimen, he works long hours, sometimes seven nights a week; never bathes, rarely shaves, and says nothing that is not spiteful. Try to discuss anything with him and you feel as if you've fallen into a cesspool. He even has the Boss beat for filthy language. And, rumor has it, he could buy out the entire fleet should he so choose. He is the owner of rattrap tenements all over town.

Many of these oldsters profess to be well-heeled, self-confessed millionaires. I have asked why they continue jouncing around town in metered jalopies, banging the hell out of their kidneys, when, according to their own

Garage mould —

The "what is it?" — atavism or mutant?

figures, they could retire in comfort on their incomes. Discounting the bluffers, these twisted fellows who get a kick out of pretended affluence, it would seem that the reason for some men working as hackies, though not pressured by fears of poverty, is an inner emptiness. They have no mental resources for leisure, nor imagination enough to tackle any other job of work.

"What am I gonna do," kidded one who admits to having a "bundle," "go home and beat up the old lady?" I looked at the cocky, stumpy, dough-complected veteran of gangfight days, when hackies wielded tire-irons in the battle for hacking privileges, when they slit tires and poured sand into gas tanks, and I understood that he wasn't kidding at all. He was *right* for this job. This was the kind of constant, senseless turmoil he needed. The cap he wore fitted his head like the dented butt of a steel wedge.

After some time on the job, I learned to spot the regulars. Even without the cap, the creased jacket and baggy pants, on his day off and dressed in his Sunday best, the stigmata of the oldtime Hackie are umistakable. First among these is his complexion. Bad eating habits, cafeteria garbage, the noxious fumes of traffic and the kidney-pounding incidental to his work have given him a face that is pasty and limp as bagel-dough. Next, his posture. He has developed a roundshouldered slouch from long jockeying, and his belly is paunchy. Most Hackies, too, grow extremely broad in the beam, thus adding

167

the washerwoman-like impression they give when talking. This talk is the ultimate giveaway. A Hackie who has by glandular good fortune escaped all the foregoing defects will, unless he is a truly strong individual, reveal himself pitiably in conversation. He will eff this and eff that, and so cover himself inescapably and irrevocably with the ordure of his bottom-dog trade. To the routine Hackie, slapped around by all sorts and conditions of men— and women—everybody in the world stinks. This is not surprising. He is merely returning an oft-repeated compliment.

MORE FRAGMENTS RELATING TO HACKING

The hackie who is respected by his fellows is the one who doesn't look it.

The man in the white suit is not interning at Bellevue necessarily; he may be selling popsicles. Likewise, the fellow who wears an Ivy League cap may never have climbed down those ivy-covered walls to go off to town on a toot. He may be a Hackie who hasn't booked 4 pounds yet, and is worried about it. The Hack Bureau, whose regulations make the cap de rigueur, is the great leveller.

Honesty is the worst policy if you are thinking of becoming rich in this business. Hackies generally are just as honest as your average citizen living in an onerous regime, but no more so.

The conventional gangster-style cap is *de rigueur* for cabbies, and that ungentle arbiter of style, the Hack Bureau, enforces this dictum ruthlessly. But every time I violate it and substitute a fedora, I get bigger tips. Apparently the passengers still prefer gentility. The only time I thought I had a square was when my passenger, a prepossessing and elderly gent, stared hard at me. Before we parted, I asked him, Wondering about the hat, Mr. ? No, he said, he just wondered how I'd lost so much weight and how different I looked without a heavy mustache. I took the license down and looked at it. I'd been riding around all night, with the dayman's picture in the slot.

People are always late when they take a cab. One doll, chief attraction of a Swing Street niteclub, was half an hour overdue for her job. When she stepped out of the cab, the manager was waiting for her under the marquee. "This is a fine time to show your face!" he yelled. She just stared at him. "Do I have to show *that*, too?" she asked.

Drunks are no problem. That is, if you can avoid them. Once a drunk asked me to take him home. "Sure, mister, where dya live?" "Shay!" he said. "You're a pretty nosey guy, aintcha? Never mind, I'll take another cab." Then there was the drunk who knew where *he* lived, but wanted to go where *I* lived. He was afraid to face his wife.

I know a hackie who is a fixture at one bar so long, when the owner sells out, he is included in the bill of sale. Kelly runs the joint now, it used to be Grogan's, and this hackie I'm telling you about is there every night from 1 A. M. to closing, rain, shine or indifferent.

He stands up at the far end of the bar with that glassy stare that comes from facing a row of bottles for five hours, and he takes a swig of rye now and then, but never says a word. He doesn't get stewed, he's never unfriendly, but you get a feeling he wants to brood in small circles around himself. So you let him be. If you watch him real careful, you'll notice he always seems to be waiting for someone. He'll look up every time the door opens, then back to the bottles again, like he's disappointed. He's always facing out to the street, and somebody told me he carries a gat. That would be stupid, because hackies are not supposed to be armed.

I can get along very nicely with half a brain on this job, thank you, but prefer to retain my full complement of kidneys. Hence you may find me any evening in the dark, to paraphrase the poet, reading neither the comics nor the sporting page, but shielded by a half-open cab door, indulging in that century-honored custom of the European: le pissoir dans la rue. Only here we call it taking a leak. This necessity of the outdoors man has even been performed at a red light, exercising one's pee-rogative (though not by me!) with passengers comfortably esconced in the rear and oblivous to all but the mad ticking of the meter. But better that way than peeis interruptus.

Which thought permits me to delve, with no special apologies to Krafft-Ebbing, into the scatalogy of this noble profession, of which there is a pro-fusion.

SHAPE-UP

Friday is the big Shape-up. The men drifting down to the waterfront garages like flies dropping on a bucket of molasses. Part-timers, old-timers, men who heard you can make a quick buck hacking on weekends. They crowd the place, overflow on the sidewalk, hang around and spit and wait their turn. Some stand as if rooted before the Despatcher's platform, trying to catch his eye, to remind him they've been waiting around a long time, too long. Others indulge in a bit of absentminded chaff or pretend to read a newspaper. They fidget and shift from one foot to the other, trying to restrain

169

a bitter impatience. All this waste of time and strength—it makes a gaping hole in a man's life.

Caged in a cell, tamed at last but still resentful, snubbing their noses against the steel bars while dreaming of wide green fields beyond. The big guys—overfleshed, corpsical products of an unhealthy milieu—remind me exactly of chained elephants rocking back and forth, swaying from side to side, little eyes gleaming fiercely, waiting for peanuts.

THE PENNY ANTE PIRATES

In some other age, they had been meat for the gallows. Poachers, pirates, highwaymen by instinct, the lust of larceny runs deep in their veins. Today's conditions offer them only the chance for some petty pilfering, lush-rolling, pimping and overcharging. Alas, they are no true barons, despite all their riotous tales (and how they love to exaggerate!) but menial serfs who abstract an odd bottle, the master's tawny port. They are the bad boys among the city's (15,000) taxidrivers, of whom they number perhaps a tenth, but give the other nine-tenths of us a big black eye.

In talk fests that cloud the air of coffeepots and garages, hackies spin tales of weal and woe in which the dollar motif predominates. "Watdo you do when you get a 5 for a 1?" And the facetious reply: "I quick roll up the winder, then I put on my thick tapping gloves, then I tap on the winder and I holler in a loud whisper: 'Come back, Larry!'"

NOTES FROM THE PENNY ANTE PIRATES

The dull, average, decent stay-at-home cabbie provides no sparkling literary material; the other kind would be, in any other age, excellent meat for the gallows.

*   *   *

Reading books, to the Hack, is a crime second only to   He wouldn't want to be found dead with one. So, very often, after picking a couple or three splendid volumes from CC's stock, I would stop in at an automat for a free paper bag to carry them back to the garage. One gets tired of the title, "Professor", when it is bestowed naturally. Being a Porkchop is bad enough; a Porkchop with bookmarks compounds a felony.

*   *   *

Notes for *Chapter VI—Nobody* . . .

". . . Too honest is no good." "What do you do when you get a 5 for a 1?" is the standard gambit. Me, I point out the customer's mistake and give

him the correct change. I'll never make a Hackie. "I always roll up the window first," explains sleepy-eyed Anton, the Butcher, "to make sure the acoustics is right. Then I put on my special, thick, tapping gloves. I tap on the winder, and holler up in a loud whisper: "Come back!"

Short-changing, overchanging, mis-reading the clock are other techniques I have never been able to learn, and therefore doomed myself to poverty. The final twist of the knife is that these   , connivers and plain crooks always get bigger tips than the incurably honest, meek, Porkchop. These skinflint passengers deserve to be taken over the hurdles by con-men cabbies, but is rarely he who mistakes the denomination of a bill. Let them affect shock at these petty larcenies. Let the HB hold up its lillywhite hands in horror, and penalize the offender unmercifully. Yet, I say that anyone who has been exposed to the provocations of parsimonious and arrogant passengers, many of whom are deadbeats and tinhorns, all of whom are social affluent, has at least a motive for retribution. But it is usually the innocent who suffer. The skinflint rarely mistakes the number on the bill he clutches. The lush, after spilling most of his gelt at the bar, talks high, wide and handsome, but he doles out small coins to the Hackie. The tinhorn, bragging of million-buck deals, pockets his change with a careless gesture, but pinches each coin with practised fingers as it drops into his pocket. The romeo bills while juliet coos, but he watches the meter like a hawk.

I have heard the classic tale of the openhanded lush so often, and told in such unvarying detail, that I must credit it to folklore rather than fact. Always in the tales this character stumbles into a parked cab, mumbles some unintelligible directions, and falls asleep. The driver races the motor, and he wakes up. He looks around, blearyeyed, asks, "Did I pay you?", and when told that he hasn't pulls off a twenty, gives it to the driver, and falls asleep again. After a while, the driver races the motor again, coughs, hollers something, but the passenger awakens, asks "Are we there yet?", is told "No, not yet," peels off another large bill, etc. This goes on, with the cab parked at the curb all the while and the flag up, until the bum is fleeced of his last bill, is assured that he has reached his destination, and stumbles out. The total of the loot varies inversely to the modesty of the narrator. You may take all such stories with a barrel of salt.

The pattern of truth is unmistakeable, and the incidents I relate herein under are true in all essentials, in my considered judgement. The procedures are authentic; the *modii operandi* are consonant with the personalities involved. I have changed only the real names of people and places, and leave any moral reflections to better men than myself.

*   *   *

Let the gods on Mt. Olympus, reformed whoremasters all, issue their five ethical pronouncements. Laboratory conditions, however, for the testing of these principles may be found only in the streets, where the . . .

*   *   *

Larceny, when accomplished without the employment of physical violence or duress, is a subject that has always entranced and convulsed the multitudes. Uproarious comedy has been written about con-men, embezzlers, . . .

*   *   *

The Mean Drunk deserves to be "taken over" by the Penny-Ante Pirate, if only because he gives the legitimate driver such a hard time. Try to help such a one and you will soon find yourself in the stew or, more correctly, in the stew's bad graces.

A BRIEF HISTORY OF
THE TAXIMETER CABRIOLET

The invention of the Taxicab, or Taximeter Cabriolet, is an incredibly ancient one, dating back even to pre-Biblical times, or the dateless past. In the days when it was known as Juggernaut, its function was the purely mechanical one of mashing pedestrians. Today this is considered a pleasant, but not particularly pecuniary by-product. The taxicab driver who admitted that he would rather clip pedestrians than passengers would be laughed right out of the Hack Bureau. He would be given a ricksha and sent into the far reaches of the Bronx, where he will either be "dimed to death", in the jargon of the trade, or fall off a cliff. A man must keep up with the trend, you know. He must put first things first, and last things last. That is nothing if not logic. Have it your way.

Peering through the mists of antiquity ("It's always bad weather when Pithecanthropi get together"), we find that the first taxicab was not a Juggernaut nor a Ricksha nor even a Hansom Cab. It was an animal named appropriately enough, the Cheetah. This experimental model carried no passengers, and could not therefore really Cheet. We deduce its position in the sequence of historic events from its passion for whizzing in and out of traffic at 80 mph and spitting at traffic cops. Unencumbered as it was with Passengers, the Cheetah developed in a healthy direction. You will hardly find one today who suffers from peptic ulcers or parking tickets. However, a few do confess to seeing spots before their eyes during the mating season. That is nature's way.

After the Cheetah, with its farfetched streamlining, automatic transmission and non-glare headlights, came the Ricksha of eternal infamy. This was equipped with a Ricksha Boy, a prototype of the modern Hackie. In functional design, fitness for his trade, including the linguistic, the former was undoubtedly superior to the latter genus. Whereas the New York, or streamlined, Hackie is confined to necessarily brief and colorless comments, such as, "I obscenity you," or "Vare gharget," his ancient Chinese counterpart was capable of such daring flights of fancy as, "I obscenity obscenity in your grandfather's goat's second cousin's obscenity obscenity obscenity." It is recorded on perishable papyrus that the first passenger subjected to this anathema, one Hung Hi, a yokel who had mooched into the big city on a tight budget, was so thoroughly dessicated by the terrible curse that he couldn't spit for a week.

The Taxicab, a Frankenstein monster with a Medallion yet, has divided modern Mankind into two distinct, conflicting races, known loosely as Hackies and Passengers. They are even, I hasten to add, joined in a great war for survival. We cannot hallow, we cannot consecrate . . . but let's wait to see who wins. Sub-species such as Pedestrians (Bipedus chowderhead), Busdrivers (Omnia gigantum), and Trailertruck chauffeurs (Absotively No Riders), are superfluous in the scheme of things, and will vanish from the face of earth as surely as the Columbus Avenue Irish or even the bison of the Great Plains. Thus the handwriting on the Thruway.

All the Speeches of
the Presidents Introduction

Throughout his adult life Herman Spector's relations with his family were strained, except with his two younger sisters . . . and his brother. Still, in his later years, he tried to explore these relations in his writing. Of particular interest are the last pieces collected here, including the poem "Artist Into Stone," pertaining to his brother. Benjamin, the eldest child, was a talented artist until a dispute with one of the older sisters ended in her destroying his paintings. The sensitive young man turned inward, stopping communication with her and his parents, the growing depression finally leading to his being institutionalized. This "crushing-to-dust of my revered brother" probably coincided with Herman's leaving high school and the world of his parents. When Benjamin died about two decades later "it was the end of something in me, the end of hope." Herman, in his writing, turned back to his childhood and the following manuscripts were among the results. The first are fragments from one approach to the autobiographical novel. The first portion of manuscript was typed in the first person and then revised to the third person, as published here. Spector's handwritten notes on the top of the first typed page comment: (in ink) "introduces My Old Man" and (in pencil) "chapter devoted to Hymie's parents and family." A second fragment uses Ralph instead of Hymie.

ALL THE SPEECHES OF THE PRESIDENTS

Hymie's father was a peasant from the fields of southeastern Europe. Transplanted to the stone jungles of Manhattan, he remained a peasant: simple, shrewd, and stubborn. Out of sheer industriousness and courage, he had carved a small niche in the stone, and hung on. He took root in the stone, he bloomed. From roustabout, machine-tender, peddler, he rose to become a tidy, busy little manufacturer. He sired a large family—four girls and two boys. He smoked expensive cigars, which he kept in an ornate humidor. He contributed to local political campaign funds. Once, a glib book-salesman succeeded in selling him a deluxe edition of "The Messages and Speeches of the Presidents." He bought a special bookcase to go with the books and fell asleep, nights, over the gravure pictures and dull text. It would have been the height of cruelty to compel him to read the books for which he had little interest and less understanding. Even as a successful businessman, he worked like a dray-horse, and had little time for reading or any other form of recreation. He would doze off at the dinner-table, and it became a jocular duty of the younger children to jog him awake, pull his shoes off, and send him lurching off to bed. Hymie's mother complained constantly of neglect, and sometimes supper was late because she had gone to a neighborhood movie with his oldest sister, Leba, to rhapsodize and weep over some emotional, "down-to-earth" tale, usually a sad one. He remembers the title of one film particularly: "The Neglected Wife," because his mother repeated it with what he thought was malicious emphasis one night, when his father roared over a late supper. If there was one thing that put the Old Man out, it was getting served late. He was a businessman, he snorted, and he wanted order and efficiency in the home as well as the shop. But order and efficiency was no safeguard against economic storms. Two years before the Depression (he was always rushing things), Hymie's father was overtaken by the tiger of bankruptcy, and transformed from a man of affairs, a mogul, a *mahka*, to a Kopsen, a *shnook*. Just a single stroke of the axe, and house, car, chauffeur, expensive cigars, and jolly "friends" vanished. Gone, too, was his wife's collection of jewelry, down to the last brooch. Mr. Rudnik was that non sequiter, "an honest businessman," and proved completely that anomolies exist, but not for long. To pay his debts he sold everything that had any value. He kept only the "Messages and Speeches," because it was impossible to find another shmoe of such dimensions anywhere in this world. He had paid $100; a Fourth Avenue dealer grudgingly offered one buck for the twenty volumes, so he chose to keep the set, lugging it with him whenever he moved, which was often.

* * *

The old man had no real humor. Although he chuckled occasionally, and snorted twice for every chuckle, and when he felt extra good might even slap you on the back, he was usually sober-serious as a man searching for a collar-button. When he relaxed, it was only behind raw clouds of smoke and large dead sheets of the *Business Opportunities* section of The New York Times. From that point of vantage, if only once, Ralph thought, he could laugh and laugh until the tears came, and he had to loosen up the belt! Essentially, he was a man with preoccupations but no enthusiasms. He was made in the conventional image of the business world. So Ralph refrained from shocking him with his own unorthodox views, or his ideas about people or books. The old man had once fallen for a slick salesman's line and stacked the shelves with twenty volumes of the speeches and messages of the Presidents, every-thing from A to Z, concluding with an index volume. He never even con-sulted them, of course: why should he? But those were all the books he would need in a lifetime. For art, he had the Remington prints clipped from National Geographic: he'd set them up in the darkest shadows of the living room, and they would last a good lifetime. In that house, Ralph walked softly and kept his own counsel.

THE WORLD OF HYMIE NUDNIK

(Editors' Note: The manuscript of these fragments for an autobiographical novel also bore the alternate titles My Old Man, All the Speeches of the Presidents and Joe Muscles.)

I

The world began on a cobblestone street set square on the crest of a hill. Down this hill the kids would sweep, screaming on fake horses, shooting accurately with finger or toy pistol, then gaily up the next block, a little winded now, and pause at the top to count captives and victims, and maybe reload and catch their breath until deciding what to do next. To the east, stretched a long series of hills culminating at Prospect Avenue, where the sky began. The air was always clear and crisp in the Bronx of those days. The creak of wagonwheeels and clop-clop of hooves were heard then more often than the rusty flatulence and klaxon-squawk of the motor cars, and empty lots for roasting "mickies" abounded. Green things grew besides the cobble-stones, plus piles of building sand and foundation walls, all just for playing and clambering on.

Hymie was four years old when the family moved here from Jennings Street. It was another step up the ladder for the Nudniks: it meant more and bigger rooms, an inside toilet, steam heat, higher rent. The street was a miracle of cleanliness.

IA.

Even the names of the streets and districts were odorous with magic in the days when I was a child in the Bronx. Van Nest, West Farms Road,

Throggs Neck, Trinity Avenue, Williamsbridge, Westchester—these were far places that beckoned and wound through one's five-fingered dreams. The source of all was a deep and liqueous gorge that lay in eternal shadow at the bottom of a hill. This was Third Avenue. The way there led from my top-floor eyrie on Crotona Parkway. Down, down smooth skateways of stone to that final grassy cliff we would clear in one glorious, swift leap. When I was older, it was the road to a palace of magic, the Public Library, Washington Avenue branch. And nothing was more perfect than a gleaming pair of Winslow roller skates. When you took them off or put them on you smelled the good smell of leather and grease and sharp machine-oil. Nothing will ever be swifter than a child on skates.

Sometimes I would journey far in the other direction, until I reached the swampland at West Farms Road. There I would cut a switch, flick it in the air to urge on an imaginary galloping steed, and whistle a warning to hidden foes.

The public school was Gothic and gray, gray slabs for the wall, gray for the steps, and a gray look in the teachers' faces. Mister Kennedy, the principal, was grayest of all.

Before we finally moved away to Brooklyn, I took a long, long hike through these familiar and mysterious streets again. I marvelled how the wondrous borough seemed to begin in liqueous darkness, in the shadowy gorge of Third Avenue, and rose and wound as a woman's body searched out by night and man's five-fingered dream, then vanished in a far drench of silence. Van Nest, Throggs Neck, West Farms, Eastchester Road, I mouthed the names again, and found them good. In memory, I cut whippy stems from the swamps, splashed about in the creek, roasted mickeys and smoked sweet, cornstalk cigarettes with carefree chums in whose young hearts no dull process of grayslab school held long tenure. This had been my boyhood, my spring; it would not come again.

THE BELOVED NEVER DIES

On the bridge:

Lookit, she said, the moon! Its mellow fullness magically rendered the outlines of tenements, transformed the hive of streets into a distant orient of joy. It's plunk in the middle of the river, she said, and her full round lips were moist with its light.

*   *   *

It was after a troubled sleep in which a dream carried over an argument, and when I got up and boiled me a cup of tay, I looked around the apartment and saw evidences on all sides of the work of her hands and heart. And I knew that it was not pity, nor habit, that kept me tied to her but, leave me face it, love, and only love. And the thought healed me at once.

*   *   *

He had taken off his jacket. Now, lying out on a rock in the park, the sun stilled all his unrest, soothing him. Sleeping, he began to groan, and groaning, he saw the beloved face again. He felt her hands stroking his breast. I want you, he groaned, and she answered. I am here, I shall never leave you. It seemed he was only sighing deeply.

*   *   *

I bounded up the steps at Essex Street and, as I reached the street level, the red afternoon sun at my back, I felt desire throbbing in me like a tiger. Every date I had with Ruth, it was the same way. The very thought of her sent flames soaring, dreams (desires) throbbing in my being. I rushed along, impatient of the crowd, thrusting my way between shoppers with packages, gesticulatory peddlers, all sorts and conditions of humans. This was Ruth's neighborhood, and it was all exciting and wonderful to me, because she lived here. I saw her standing in a space between the theatre display and a candy-store counter; her dark eyes burned into mine, and only the knowledge that we were on a thronged street prevented us from seizing the moment for an embrace. As it was, I would not even touch her. I mumbled something about coming late, I hoped she hadn't been waiting long.

*   *   *

East-Side Girl
As Lisa waits at darkened window of flat, looking down on moving masses in grease-flaring east side pushcart street, recapitulates in swift, incisive strokes of memory-flashes her background, mores, wounds, home-life, parents, early trauma, introduction to underworld of lover for whom she is waiting: mingled feelings of apprehension, lechery, joy, hopelessness. it is a spring evening, 1926.

Walking amid throngs and responding to color in street is Joseph, innately restless, approaching crisis in his life. admirer of the "hardboiled" school, abandoning academic pursuits yet not at all really concerned about chief motivation of the land, money; luxuriates in the poetry which constantly germinates in him, as does sexneeds which torment him at this stage.

*   *   *

The first time I saw her, it was as if a flame leaped into life, illumining her eyes and hair, and I saw nothing else. She was standing at the end of a long work-table, packing leather belts neatly and expertly into white paste-board boxes. The shop foreman nudged me. "Come on," he said, "I'll show

179

Spector's last drawing of his wife, done from his hospital bed

you the cutting tables." But I wasn't listening. In a moment, she looked up and saw me there. She flushed, and turned away. In that moment I was seared with desire for her, but something more than desire restrained me from speaking. I was incapable of saying anything flippant; the mood was too perfect to spoil. There was no time, either, for groping inanities. I turned and followed the foreman out.

"Not a bad hunk of fluff, huh?" he winked at me. Ordinarily, the remark would mean very little, but now it rankled. He was ten years older than myself, a sharp-featured fellow with thinning hair, factory pallor, and an air of covetousness. "Why do you say that?" I inquired, coldly. "Or is that your opinion of all the girls here?" Crazy, I thought to myself, what am I giving him guff for? It was going to be important for me to have good relations with the shop—that is, if I wanted my orders delivered on time. This was my first job selling on the road, and here I was, lousing it up.

"No harm meant, kid," he joshed, "I know you travelling guys are always looking around. If you like her that much, I'll give you an intro. She's new here, too."

But I was all business from then on. Sure, he'd give me a knock-down, then tell the boss I was fooling around with the inside "help." And that would get the girl in trouble, too. No, thanks. I was young, but I wasn't green. I finished the tour, which was to familiarize me with the factory set-up, then I spent the rest of the day helping the foreman whip up the last of my samples. It was the firm's new spring line, and as I fingered the bright leathers and buckles, I thought of the raven-haired beauty behind the partition. In three days, I'd be on that Chattanooga choochoo . . . I was determined to know her a little better by then.

"You know the business pretty good for a youngster," the foreman said, with just a hint of condescension. "Where'd you learn it?"

"Since I was twelve years old," I grinned, "I've been hopping around belt factories—mostly my father's. I used to help out on Saturdays and after school."

"Oh, the boss's son, eh?"

LISA'S FATHER

The slight quirk of his pale grey eyes, the high flat cheekbones, the wisp of moustache in the thin, gaunt face gave him the appearance of a mandarin. When he spoke, slowly and softly but with emphasis, his lips curled disdainfully, his words bore the unction of a personality which could not possibly conceive itself in the wrong. The shoulders were narrow and hunched, the head on its fragile stem of neck was cocked forward, making him look like a professor awaiting questions from the class. He smoked cigarettes through a long holder, was careful about the ashes, had acquired a deftness in blowing smoke through his nostrils to punctuate his remarks. In his manners and speech, in his pronouncements on people and affairs, he strove to imitate the grand airs of a Viennese boulevardier, that *luftmensch* type which he still revered. In the company of his peers he was sedate, reserved, and leisurely. He had the reputation of a *blatta*, a sophisticate, a man-of-the-world. But with women, and especially with younger women, the courtly air descended to music-hall impertinences. He would allude to sex with obvious double-entendres, with remarks which had their origin in some secret frustration, since the amatory propensities he hinted at was not in evidence. Alone with his wife, he was carelessly correct but always querulous. Even though she obeyed in all things with the swift submissiveness of a slave, her obedience seemed to come from some tyrant within, and his voice acquired an almost pleading tone, betraying his knowledge of this automatism.

THE CITY'S CHANGED

Ah, the Old East Side! I mean the really old, absolutely East, not side of ham, not side of bacon, not eggs sunnyside but side of Henry, *matjes* with a tsibilla thrown in it—watch it! Ah, the good-old-timers of Chrystie Street, Norfolk, Suffolk, Orchard, Ridge, Pitt, and all the rest! The shouts of deliverance, the whistles of *shamuses*, the steaming odors of sacrifice! Shoppers and peddlars in open combat in the crowded, littered lanes, mixing-it-up with gusto, so that a blend of raucous insult emerges, delivered while pawing, poking, snatching and catching at scraps and oddments of dubious merchandise to confuse the very gods of commerce and travail. A beggar's opera spoken or chanted, screamed or sung, but played out to the last note, the very last syllable, by players in motley who never lost their zest or muffed a cue (alt., forgot their lines): "Ahya, ahya, ahya! Alla gutta zocken! Nemt a shtickel, a shtickel for a nickel—here lady, don't pick em, eida you buy or you don't buy but *don't touch*—gaw head, so help me it cost me more—awright, tree cents, fertig! Ahya, ahya, ahya!" And in the butcher shops, the whiskered slaughterers and slicers slapping away with cleavers and knives, plucking out feathers, sawing through bones. Sawdust and chicken-feathers. Fat carp and flatfish, butterfish on the fishmonger's scale, gleaming with blood and slime, slapped up and wrapped up in newspapers. Indian-nuts and watermelon seeds shovelled into bags . . . and the bobbas in sheitels and shawls.

*   *   *

THE CHICKEN-SLAUGHTERER

Never will I forget the simple joys of Matzos-time in old Haarlem-bruick! Amid the shouts of deliverance, the whistles of shamuses, the steaming odors of sacrifice: snotnosed elders, wet behind the ears, running in and out of jerry-built salamanders. Cossacks hanging from the rafters, their half-baked brains spewing a crimson jetty of repentance on to the candycoated tiles. Chicken-feathers, with sawdust choking the oyster beds. A chiarivari of *fashiddina zacken*, whirling in mad abandon while staid publicans look on reproachfully. "A shaina gashickta," my Uncle Nuchim mutters into his beard while hobbling to the comparative safety of the bullpen. There, while a

182

toreador in full phylacteries koshered the meat with antique blade and stampeding herds thundered into rooms of self-service abbattoirs, he pored over the words in the dread Kabbala: "And a morain shall devour them entire; and all their butt-rumped magnificence shall come to naught; and their children's children unto the last generation alas also." The language was designedly obfuscate, multi-adjustable and eternal. My Uncle Nuchim was even such a man: he considered that anything in print must be sacred, else it would not have paid to print it. He would not even use a newspaper for the outhouse, as the others did.

IN THE NICKELODEON*

SATURDAY EVENINGS WERE PURPLE WITH CIGAR-SMOKE, and yellow with electriclights and laughter. The womenfolk bustled about, and chattered, making a great to-do over the meats and garnishes, pastries and tea. They streamed in and out of the swinging door, trailing from living room to kitchen in an unending procession. My mother was an excellent cook; we kids snatched up what we liked, ran through the rooms of the flat like figures in a Keystone comedy. Then the men, having stuffed themselves, hurried the women to clear off the dishes. Then the big circular table was pulled out, and the center leaves inserted, new decks of cards brought out and snapped open and stacks of bright-colored chips counted out. The poker session, the big event of the evening, was on in earnest.

(or)

. . . In evenings purple with cigarsmoke, yellow with laughter and electric lights, and the to-and-fro bustlings of womenfolk serving refreshments and offering advice, Fat Joe opens the round with a double bet—2 nickels— and another big pot begins to add up. Benny is there, trying to get that Buster Keaton look on his lanternish features; and Uncle Moish, squinting and croaking commands to his harassed daughters; and Big Hymie, swinging around in his chair like a goodhumored sloth to wink at us kid-kibitzers and indicate exactly where the loot is to fall. They always play poker on the great, circular leaf-table in the front room, and Little Hymie and me are very glad of that, too, because the table never can be made to shut perfectly when that leaf is in, and there are two nice wide cracks, one on each side of it, where a stray nickel, dime, or even quarter gets mysteriously lost. When Big Hymie plays, there's nothing mysterious about it.

Big Hymie is the tallest of my big-cousins, not as old as Fat Joe, but much nicer. Like Fat Joe and Benny, his cousins, he is a cabdriver, but wears

*Also titled "In a Silent Movie (The Clutching Hand Fills a Straight Flush)" or "The Pinochle of Success."

his cap more jauntily than they. He has a kid brother, too, but I never see him and never could remember his name to this day. They play for the kicks, for the money, for the noise, for the prestige of the winner.

Little Hymie, my cousin, pale and dull; lean, silent always, pretty much bullied by older brothers—friendly, a follower in all things, in some ways precociously more.

And sitting at the head of the table, smiling, jovial, the perfect friendly host, my father—urging them to stay, as if he himself did not have to wake at 4:30 A.M. and put in another 14 hour day. The swirl of smoke, the patter, chatter, the gusto with which they devoured the food—always a healthy spread laid out, and lots of delicatessen, pickles, tea, honeycake—then the farewells, the butt-strewn table, dishes piled high—my mother and sisters cleaning up. Then snooze all . . . my father as always the loser . . . the front room shuttered and dead.

THE BRONX

THE BRONX WAS A DELIGHTFULLY BUMPY, vast playground for kids. A place of steep, sudden hills, of far vistas, of stretches of sandy lots and weedy woodlands. Gangs of us would rage out of   apartment dwellings, fronted by checkerboard pavement and cursed with unfriendly supers, to find adventure in wild chases, in long hikes and wide-ranging games of ringalevio or prisoner's base. In the afternoons we boiled around the block with softballs, racing on skates, pedalling uphill and coasting down again. From time to time, our moms would wail down from the windows, and we'd holler back. Grateful gifts of pennies wrapped in paper, or jellysand-wiches, plunked to the sidewalk to punctuate the regular course of our play. Or a dictatorial errand would cast its gloom over us.

*   *   *

THEN TWILIGHT WOULD COME, DEEPENING the outlines of buildings, and soon the lamplight would fall like snowdust through the purple cone of sky. I hear the strains of the old, dimly remembered song my brother played on his fiddle. And as I listen, I discern the architecture of a certain street, now altered or completely vanished, where we played and laughed in the fantasy-life of childhood. I walk in areas of mist, where only the clicking of my heels is heard. Except for an occasional whining of a trolley, or . . .

*   *   *

TRINITY AVENUE, The Bronx. (Pictures, smells, images)
ringalevio games under lamplight
peddlar's horses, cobblestone curb, ice wagon lunch.

jellyapp; lollipops, licorice, schmaltz on rye
spunky shrunken little tailor and kid
old house supposed to be haunted—telling ghoststories on steps
toy houses on long Street—skating
warm summer eves—fresh hot jelly donuts from dutch bakery
campchairs in front of billboard   under lite
Crotona Parkway kids doing cardtricks and magic
animals Bronx Park Zoo—long walks—cycling
hymie (pale) and the clutching hand—9 o'clock curfew
fat joe (dog) and benny (whining voice), cabbies
sisters, silent Sadie and Bella
uncle morris—severe from meaning naught
tanta   —slicing bread held against belly with cleaver
Lebo clan—autos—motorcycle
Sam, Mac, Al, Moe, parents Syrian type, the women they married

*   *   *

(Bronx-Atmosphere streets: 1910-15)

Trinity Ave.—163rd St. locale—corner saloon with swinging doors—
greengrocers with awning and open barrels—kids swiping apples, spuds,
chased by fresh-cheeked clerk—little bald tailor (Tannenbaum)—"tough"
kids—Angelo, the Burke twins, Stine—mean hoodlums. Afternoons of sun-
light on cobblestones, gingerbread houses with sunken entrances, steps going
down—streetlamp lit by old Italian with long pole over shoulder—twilight
and street games: Ring-a-levio, Prisoner's Base, Red Rover Come Over, etc.
Roasting mickies on big bonfires in empty lots, scrambling over sand
mounds, foundation walls of buildings in construction—kid who stepped in
wet (hot) cement—chewing tarballs—street gangfights—hustling balls of
manure (Angelo), antisemitic bullies—the hills, hitching rides on icewagons,
skating, whizzing around corners, sleigh-riding. Afternoons—roasted chest-
nut vendors, (sweet potato venders downtown only)—open political rallies,
soapboxes—open-air movies under the stars in warm weather—amateur pics
outside of customers—to be shown following week—pratfalls—the "haunted
house" . . .

*   *   *

IN THOSE DAYS, MY MOTHER had a way of not smiling, like a
night of no stars, when you are suddenly left standing alone and know your-
self to be lost, irrevocably, lost in an endless darkness wherein vague terrors
are to be found in each clump of bushes, behind each tree. Then I would stop
whatever I had been doing, and all things in my 9-year universe would come
to a dead halt, and wait for me to catch up. "Wassamatter, Mom?" I would
ask, trying to find the answer in her eyes.

185

"Greena jobba!* Go to sleep already!"

I could never sleep at night. The dark was too lived in.

I swallowed the dark. I was small for my age, but in the dark, I was King. Poor Mom had no happiness from her brood. "I hope to see *nachas* from you some day," she'd say, wistfully. But she loved my brother Ben the best, because he was the first-born. And that's natural, isn't it, for that's the way it stands in the Bible: favor the first-born. Only, he got sick and she wouldn't want anyone to know.

*Green Devil (translation)

*   *   *

TWENTY-FOUR HOURS IS THE size of the clock. It has turned twice when it clicks, and a low chirr begins. This is the clock of the bronze Napoleon, whose gleaming sword I had so often unscrewed, to admire under the glittering lights of the chandelier. Now the living room is dark; it is twilight outside the drawn shades. My brother sits quietly, his hands folded, gripped in the ritual of defeat. He is pale, withdrawn, his gray eyes fixed upon a point in space. Through the room pass, unnoticed, the other members of the family: mother, sisters, myself . . . We no longer speak, we are figures moving noiselessly through his dream. At the table, as we dine together, he places a hand over his eyes and shuts us out of his secret world.

OLD FOLKS AT HOME

Reaching the door, he waited, listening. It was too late to pay a visit. But they kept late hours nowadays. The old man might be dozing off in the big armchair just in time to miss Gabriel Heatter, his mother busied with some last-minute chore—or huddled near the radiator in a far corner. He pressed closer. There was not a sound. Perhaps they were both asleep, weaving dreams of happiness from their sorrows, dreams that had neither beginning nor end. He sighed, then let himself in with the key his mother had given him, that night he came over to say that he had separated finally from Estelle.

"Any time you want, Yummey, you should come over. Take from the icebox. I wish you could stay here at least till you get settled. But my nerves . . ." And his father, cranky but only meaning to make things good for everybody: "Why don't you call up at least every day, let us know how you're getting along? Is this too much trouble for a son? Only a nickel, it costs. You know how your mother worries; so keep in touch!" . . . As if he were still a kid, instead of a man of forty with partial dentures and graying hair. He would always be their son, their *ainchicka*, their only one. Despite anything he could do, they enfolded him with their warm, cloying affection. They were spinning a second cocoon for the butterfly shorn of its wings . . .

The sound of the door closing behind him caused his father to wake with a start. The old man, as usual, had dozed off after supper, seated at the big chair. He lifted a haggard, thin-edged face, and stared up at him with red-stained eyes. What was he thinking? White strands of hair mussed his smooth brow. The square jaws jutted from the corded neck. It was the face of a fighter who knew he was licked, but fought on hopelessly.

"What's new, Pop?"

For a moment the face returned nothing, neither welcome nor pleasure, and it seemed the old man would drop off to sleep again. Then, with an effort, he pulled his body up straight in the chair and stretched his stiffened legs. "Yummey? So, sit down, Yummey. We didn't expect you so late." The voice came from far away.

The lamps were all lit in the living room; it was warm there, and cozy. A high, elliptical mirror, a reminder of the larger house they had once owned, over the sideboard, the dark wood tea-chest, the bulbous, ornamented floor-lamp, all bespoke distant, more opulent times. Yummey felt his age like a stab. These were the trappings of the nest he had flown at nineteen. The folks looked exactly the same, but his parents were old, broken, weighed down with his failures and disappointments. Never had they received *nachas* from him. He knew now that they never would.

"Where's Mom?"

The old man craned toward the closed bedroom door. "Momma," he called, almost jovially. "Yummey is here." Turning back again, he explained, "Momma isn't feeling so hot. She's laying down. But you wait. She'll come out right away, don't worry. Take your coat off." His son made no motion to obey. Instead he waited, tensely. He had always known this tension in the presence of his parents. Even as a child, it was something made him hold back, wait, and in the waiting there was both pity and fear. Yes, he would always be afraid. Afraid of what? Of hurting someone? His parents? Himself? He sweated. It was very warm in the room, but he stubbornly decided not to remove his overcoat.

"What are you doing nowadays?" Even his voice betrayed the fear he could never wholly suppress. He wanted to make conversation, to dispel the fog of the unreal atmosphere.

"What should I do?" The old man shrugged. "Nothing with nothing. I run here, I run there. Everybody gives promises. Next week, next month, three months. Whenever the season should start up. Who knows?"

Fear was clawing at his throat now. His eyes went very wide. This was his father, once a vigorous, successful businessman, wielding both authority and power. This man was a legend in the ladies' pocketbook field. The old-timers and their sons, all knew him. "That's Spiegel. One of the biggest men in the industry at one time. Smart. Knows the business inside out. Today he just *potchkes* around, makes himself up a few samples, tries to get orders. I like to give him a help, why not, but what I'm gonna do? When it's slow by me, I don't need nothing. When it's busy, I need in a hurry. Naah, he ain't got no shop, no workers, no machines, nothin! A *luftmensch*!

Yes, they all knew this bent, pitiful figure. And they were all so well-meaning, respectful, salvaging their consciences. They let themselves be buttonholed in lobbies, they let him take up their valuable time. "Believe me, Mr. Spiegel, I know you can make up a pocketbook." Later, to an associate, they would brag about their generosity. "Know who I ran into today? Spiegel. The old man. For his age, he looks pretty good. Still runs around like a youngster. How does he do it?" And they would think: "Yes, a fine old man. It should never happen to me." And rarely one might speculate: "Hear he's got a son he won't talk about. In the jewelry line, a manager or is he a salesman? Anyhow, a fellow who'll let the old man burn out his strength, I got no use for. What kind of person is it, what kind of a feeling for a father?"
. . .

It was very warm in the room. Why did they keep the windows closed so tightly all the time? "No, don't open no windows, Yummey. Your mudder catches cold too easy." Everything was too neat, clean, orderly. The timid arrangement of fruit bowl and Sunday papers irked him, gave him a feeling of despair. Is this the way things go on and on and on forever, without protest, without meaning, without understanding. He was a stranger here. He felt his breath come sharply. Then he looked up, and saw his mother standing in the archway.

She was a figure salt-sad, rigid, white, Lot's wife returned to the living land, reproach, not to God but to man. She beamed wanly on Yummie with her single eye.

"Yummey, how are you?" A cotton patch taped the empty socket, and he could not restrain a shudder, seeing her like this. It was years ago, years now that she had suffered the loss. And for years before, the agony, the hope of saving it, the maltreatment of moneygrubbing quacks. Now she held the glass eye hidden under the towel, with the bottle of antiseptic. She passed into the bathroom. But she had been prepared for bed, and now she would have to replace the eye in its socket because he had come unexpectedly. A pattern was set: in this small flat she was unable to make a graceful entrance, to observe the *nacches* she so desired. She was a modest person. It made him want to sob, that all their lives had come to barrenness, to mutilation, to poverty without end. He ground his jaws and a hard knot grew at the pit of his stomach. If this were hysteria, then this is what things had been building up to.

His father, anyhow, puttering at the radio, was prosaically reassuring. The wave of anxiety subsided a little and left him. He relaxed.

"Pop," he grinned, "You're looking to get the news from Gabriel

Heatter? It's the same old thing. Today is just like yesterday, isn't it? So, why bother with the news broadcast?"

"No, I gotta listen to Winchell. He's on in a few minutes. This week, it's an important one."

"Like what, for instance?"

"I don't know, I don't know." The old man was grouchy. He disliked having to explain. Last week, the brassy commentator had promised to reveal something or other. That's all. Plain enough, he would say, as a way of ending arguments. Obviously, it was worth listening. Nobody ever questioned his smallest acts like this son of his. If he had only listened like other sons, when there was time yet, instead of asking why, what, who, he might be somewhere today . . . successful, a *mensch*, even happily married . . . Suddenly, the old man no longer cared to hear the news. He switched off the radio, and sat in the armchair again. Rubbing his cheek thoughtfully, he looked at his son and considered how he might somehow help him.

"You didn't get a job yet?"

"No. I chase after everything in the want ads, but so far, nothing turned up. A man of my age, without a trade . . ."

"Your age? What's the matter, you an old man already?"

"To the people who hand out jobs, yes."

*   *   *

(Editors' Note: The preceding fragment is from a partial novel, also called "Justice for All" and "The Belt People" by Spector, based on his parents' family life. Although the father in the novel had been in the ladies' pocketbook field the latter title refers to the business of Spector's father. Years after he gave up the thought of a novel on the topic he toyed with it—again as "The Belt People"—as a subject for a television play. His outline for that included the following:)

"Old man who has bankrupted in biz where he once was a big shot, never reconciled to lower eco.-social status, buttonholes cronies & is always put off, comes home to find that son & daughters arranging for him to go into Old Folk's Home—he runs away, to find solace with his 'belt people', (give at least 3 interviews with contrasting personalities) but learns that in absorption with biz, biz, all the time, he has forfeited love of family (son).

"Theme: old man's recrimination of son's previous unwillingness to become business associate with him and thus avert bankruptcy and subsequent ruin of both—finds truth at last to be other than he thought and that silent, long-suffering son never wished to bring to light . . .

"Old Man's Mistake: He preferred his 'business world' to becoming friend of son.

"Son's Mistake: He chose to be standoffish instead of trying to understand old man."

A CHILDHOOD MEMORY

I have looked for a Messiah all my life without realizing it, but never looked in the right place. The Passover seder, with its ritual of the full glass of wine set out for the bidden guest, and the unlatched door, was tremendously impressive to me as a child. I held my breath, and waited. Then attention was directed to something else, and later, suddenly, we children were told that Elenooree, the Messiah, had stolen into the room unawares and sipped from the glass; and we half-believed it. We wanted to believe in the ghostly visitor, in the joyful deliverance from slavery and evil, for somehow, though the shackles rested lightly enough upon our wrists, we felt that we were enslaved. In all, the tales of Moses, of Samson, of Rachel and Haman and all the rest, there was hardly a figure powerful enough to inspire reverence, and only Elenooree remained and he really did nothing, and was nothing. The active practise of a religious ethic, its flowering in deed—that was nowhere to be seen, nobody even discussed it. The only thing that kept the aura of separateness alive was the accounts revealing active hatred and prejudice from the other side.

When the battle is joined, the struggle of a people is one thing; it is something else again when peace reigns and the warring factions are welded into a single community. To carry aloft the tattered and bloodied standards then, when the foes are reconciled, if not as brothers, then as mutually respecting neighbours, is not only silly; it is destructive. So I could not mouth the words that meant separateness, even had I understood them. Knuckle-rapping at Cheder could not instill in me the fanaticism of the ghetto Jew. I had no use for it at all. The creed had no meaning for me. . . .

Much, much later I found a figure with whom I could be consanguineous, in whom I could believe. This was not so much a figure as the embodiment of all I hold good in human personality. Because the figure moves me in such a way, it is greater than the greatest art. Because it inspires me with inconquerable love, it embraces all other loves. And, finally, because it leads me to understanding, it is a knowledge further than all others, which are fragments of a truth.

(Editors' Note: This memory fragment was written, as were many of these unpublished pieces, on the pages of a 3 by 5-inch spiral notebook. It ended at this point. Since Spector normally covered every bit of whatever paper on which he wrote, and this piece stopped in the middle of one of the tiny pages, he apparently never got further with the description/explanation of this figure.)

REMEMBERING HIS MOTHER

I

Under the bedclothes there seemed to be nothing intelligible. Yet how strong the narrow fingers that gripped mine, and with what disdain her eyes looked at me. The downpull of old thin lips expressed ancient grief. "Harry," she called hoarsely, but still peremptorily. "Do you have seven dollars?" It was an official rather than a plea. I told her I didn't. "Bring it. I'll need another intravenous tomorrow. Now go, you must go to your job," she said.

How she had, with stubborn fierceness, fought for her supremacy! Her judgments had to avail against the world's. Consideration for the integrity of others had no place. Yes, she it was who destroyed my brother. How she had masterminded Belle's foolish, vain marriage. How she had curbed and curtailed the life and vision of Mimi. How she tried to straitjacket and castrate me—as unwilling synagogue-attender, as her private chauffeur—and how she had ripped my marriage at the seams.

Stripped of all marks, all nonessentials, she was seen in her long agony of dying and despair, as the bitter personification of a folk-myth that the sacrifice of the child to the parent results in happiness and salvation. To compensate for the hurts she had received at the hands of a sadistic older sister, the mother became actively malignant at the time of her menopause.

Then, Mimi was an adolescent and needed social contacts and expressions of her own needs, and was dragged into this vortex of self-sacrifices only

191

to repudiate it when it was too late, thus continuing and extending the injury to brothers, husband and child. Then, Harry had reached young manhood, and his choices were frustrated in advance. . . .

Who has the heart (he reflected, looking down at that pitiable wreck of a body) to say the things that hurt the old, yet need so much to be said? She shall die beyond hope and beyond reason. You cannot touch her with the stickly rod of truth now. Nor remind her that religion never really was a solace, never was more than an instrument of vanity and hypocrisy. She is, and always was, deluded. So she thought that the "sacrifice" of motherhood was something to be repaid? Poor, deluded, wretched, betrayed soul!

Surely, he thought, there must be a better way to die. But how, after a lifelong acceptance, false hopes, beliefs, values? This was a soul betrayed by god and man. A bitter curse lay on her . . . the blindness and the   of the persecuted. While murderers revel throughout the land, the naive, the poor, are shriveled by fire. She was a kind, decent woman after all. She lived worthily, after her fashion. She drudged and slaved against the evil web of circumstance, against the   of a foe she could not name, not for herself merely but for the family so dear to her, which yet served her so badly.

Now he saw how all her life had passed in agony and disappointments that left their marks and wrinkles in her face. Dying now, she was cantankerous and weak. It was as if all the contradictions, all the fears, all the poisons accumulated during her long travail had come to a festering head and only at intervals, between crying spells and words of self-pity, she had clumsy, fleeting glimpses of the truth. She saw the dust settle over the hopeless ruins of the family, and there was no city. There would never be a city.

II

IN THOSE DAYS MY MOTHER had a way of not smiling, like a night of no stars, and I would know that she was thinking about Yummey, my elder brother. Suddenly, I would be lost in a jungle of impenetrable darkness, a vastness peopled by vague shapes of terror. Then everything would stop in my 9-year-old world, and I would enter into that strange world of my mother's, that world of worry and silence. Her voice would become subdued, and lost, and trail off into a mysterious silence that pervaded all the house, particularly the furniture.

The furniture always partook of her mood. When she was brooding, like this, the bed always had a sleepy, faraway look; the bureau and sideboards assumed a tremendous dignity; and the massive, overstuffed chairs in the living room became maned lions, bigger than any in the zoo, crouched and ready to spring. Wandering about the house, I avoided the living room with a shudder, but I loved to stand and watch the deep shadows moving in the depths of that magic pool that was the dining room mirror. I thought I might find there in its shimmering well the source of the sadness that had overcome my mother, and subjugate it to my will. But I never could. So, lacking any words of courage or knowledge to lay in her lap, I would return to where she sat, hunched and stiff, and pull down a hand from her face, and ask, "What's the matter, Mom?" She rarely answered, but I was comforted by the larger warmth and sturdiness of her hand, and thus reassured, would fly down the six flights to the street, whooping like an Indian and clutching a chunk of pumpernickel deliciously moistened with chicken-fat. Thus had I dispelled all mists, and merged myself with the life of the kid gang of which I was then a proud member.

THE PARTY WILL CALL BACK

(Editors' Note: Spector left two unfinished versions of this story, also called "A Walk in the Snow" or "The Canvasser's Story," as well as his synopsis or story line. The latter is printed here, followed by the two versions.)

Synopsis:
    Tragedy of a little man—
    Told in 1st person narration.
begin facing side pages. . . .
tells how, going out to canvass—with crew—describe: Snydr (the Brite), Jonesy (the slick operator)—make merchandise he is selling purposely vague and meaningless. Use science-fiction term (plexidrops or plextron, the scientific, all-control, push-pull necessity which no home should be without). bad conscience about the price, too—in town where figures emerge out of his dim past, he is impelled back to childhood—sees brother again—hears the violin song—when he comes to, he is back in city and it is twilight—misses sample case of gleaming plexitron, goes by instinct to customary restaurant—mechanically orders in a   —waitress reminds of wife from whom he has separated—brief recap here telling of his unfortunate marital experience,   futility of following will of possessive mother—at moment of violent scene (with mother) phone in booth rings, waitress is holding to ear and calling his name—which, of course, she doesn't know—he answers—strange conversation ensues—broken off at high point, when he is attempting explanation of everything—operator's mechanical assurance, "the party will call back." he goes outside, after being stopped for payment of check—and stared at meanly by all—sits on bench and reflects fearfully as snow begins to fall

VERSION A

I need to tell someone, and it may as well be you. Since it happened—almost a week ago—I've been restless, jumpy, unable to sleep more than an hour or two at a time. My friends tell me I look terrible; they ask

193

what's the matter, but I can't tell them without making myself out to be an utter idiot. It's bad enough they look upon me as a failure, a frustrated artist, a man of uncertain talents and indefinable charm. I surely don't want them to think of me as a candidate for the booby hatch.

I've been busting with the urge to tell it all to someone sympathetic, someone who won't or can't just walk away and laugh, and say, Well, that's the way it is in New York, it's a city of crackpots. . . .

It's true that living in furnished rooms for a long time does something to a man. He comes and goes like a ghost. The landlady may notice him, but only as a necessary nuisance, something lacking the vital spark and the of a human being, yet not quite as loveable or useful as a household pet. "You left your key in the door this morning," she admonished me last week. "I warn you, I won't be responsible if anything is missing." Well, who cares? Thieves can take away anything they like in my room: none of it has even a sentimental value. I am a man whose present, past, future, have long since vanished into insignificance. But an incident that took place last Friday night in the S & H cafeteria, which puzzles me, and makes me afraid . . . What does it mean? Am I about to be reborn? Shall I die very soon? If I only knew the answer. . . .

Since I shifted quarters from the fussy little house in Flatbush (where things were even too straitlaced to suit a middleaged bachelor like myself), to the noisy and dangerous environs of the upper West Side, I have been dining fairly regularly at the S & H. This is a little Viennese place where the food is not too good, but is cooked with something like decent care. Mostly refugees eat there. I do not much care for these people, who seem to have learned not at all from their sufferings. They represent only the beagle-eyed bourgeoisie, I believe, and not the real masses of these countries ruined by the scourges. If not for the accident of "race," who knows? They might have turned out to be perfect little nazis themselves. But this is another matter, not at all germaine to the happening of which I will tell.

First, I must explain something of my predicament. A middle-aged gentleman of sedentary habits; not a profligate, not a drunkard, who is always broke, who is alway jumping from one uncertain job to the other, must require some documented story to defend his bitter lot. Well, I have none. I was born into a most piddling middle class family, dropped my studies when still in high school, and drifted. I married early and badly. The rest is simply a horrible mess of confusion compounded with misery. Recently I agonized through my forty-fourth birthday. Yes, I said to myself, I am middleaged. I have been unhappy and unsuccessful all my life. If I have known love at all, it has been a blasting, searing, hateful sort of love. I have not even attempted any great deeds. I volunteered in no wars. I have been free with criticism and chary of creations. That is the way I castigate myself on occasion, and the last birthday was indeed a mournful occasion.

194

All the same, I set out bright and early of that day to work at my financially hazardous and not at all dignified occupation. My friends believe that I am a regular salesman. When they question me as to what I am selling, I tell them "general merchandise," and they nod sagely. One of these fellows with a faulty connection, they reason. They pity me, sometimes. They tell me to go up to see Mr. Whozis, who might decide to place me in a fairly decent job but who never does. Or they tell me to fill auntie's application for a civil service job, or scour the papers more thoroughly for business opportunities, or why the hell don't I just take up bookkeeping or tailoring at night? Actually, I am a canvasser, a doorworker, a fellow can't do any more than ring a bell, deliver a formulated spiel, and depart. Doesn't matter what a canvasser canvasses: he is never going to make any money at it, he is never going to rise out of the injustice and the mockery of this miserable trade. You have seen the winos on the Bowery, the creatures who once allegedly were men: they will never return to life, they are lost. And so it is with the canvasser.

On the morning of which I would speak, I decided to canvass on Long Island, in Manhasset, For no special reason. Perhaps I dreamed of finding "virgin territory" in that town—a canvasser always dreams of finding something fresh, of slicing into "cream cheese." I purchased my ticket at the 34th Street depot, settled down with a N. Y. Times, and dozed throughout the ride.

The day was gloomy, gray, and threatened rain. A young canvasser, full of piss and vinegar, wouldn't mind that at all. At 44, I was an old, tired, firehorse who should have been retired long ago. I clumped up the wooden steps to the street, and looked upon the world sourly.

Strange . . . A cabbie, with a smashed-in face was waiting in his cab at the curb. He looked strangely familiar, like someone met in the wilds of Brooklyn. I couldn't place him, and it wasn't important. I tossed . . . . . .

VERSION B

It had been sunny all afternoon. When night came, Mr. Spiegel was sitting at his customary table at the S & H Restaurant where he is an anonymous silent guest who tips little and is somehow disliked. This certain evening, while Mr. Spiegel is ruminating on the futility of his life, the sad vaudeville of his occupation, the frustration of all his talent and hopes, the meal is interrupted by the insistent ringing of the phone in the booth nearby. A waitress answers: there is no one at the other end. Puzzled, she hangs up. The phone rings again. Mr. Spiegel gets a funny feeling that this call is for him. But nobody knows him here. He continues to eat the not so relished food. The phone rings again. He gets a strong impulse to answer, but controls it. This time the waitress, a determined, masculine wench, picks up the phone angrily. She has a little difficulty in hearing. She comes out with a dazed look: Is there a Mr. Spiegel here? There ought well be, but except for our hero, there doesn't seem to be. Nobody knows him here, nobody he knows would know of this restaurant, so who would be calling? Timidly, he acknowledges his identity and goes to the phone. He picks up the receiver. Timidly, he says, "Hello. Who's this?"

"You know who this is," a voice snaps. It is the deliberately assured voice of his mother, a grand dame, a ruler of destinies. She goes on to castigate him for keeping her waiting.

"What is it you want?", he wonders.

"I gave you all the opportunities," she says scornfully, "but you failed in everything. You failed me, you failed your father, you failed your sisters, you failed your wife, you failed your brother."

"No!" He peremptorily stops her there. "Everyone else I failed. But I did not fail my brother. I want to bring to your recollection a certain incident."

"What incident?" She is uncertain, not so positive now.

"You know very well. The incident in the snow. A walk in the snow."

"I don't know what you're driving at."

He tells her. How, as a child, he was asked to snitch on his brother, to tell information about the the wild company his brother had presumably fallen in with, how he was to trail him one late afternoon and report. He had followed his brother through blocks and blocks in the Bronx. A snow began to fall. The world was transformed. The lights glowed through a purple , softening golden flakes on the white world. The park. And the meeting and understanding with his brother. The walk as comrades. The return. The violin. . . .

As he tells this, it all becomes magically entwined with the lost past and a somehow golden future. Meanwhile, someone wants to use the phone and is glaring at him through the panel, stomping back and forth. He doesn't care, he ignores the hatred blithely, takes his time.

But his mother finally stops the story. Becomes tearful. He cannot take this without inward weeping. With a great , he realizes his mother is dead 10 years, his brother 12. (She was killed by grief.) She ends in denouncing him again, and saying "You never should have been born. I want to tell you that I am calling you back." (*Herman's note:* Make above happen prior to his expostulation.)

They seem to be cut off. He appeals to operator. "But she could not have hung up!" he declares (*Herman's note*: does not realize till after leaves booth that mother is long dead!)

Operator is courteous but grossly indifferent. "Do you know the number the party was calling from? No? Well, perhaps the party will call you back. Sorry, I can't help you. The party will call you back."

196

He leaves booth. Confused, angry, upset, overwhelmed. What fate is in store for him? Will he die? Will his mother "call back?" (Windup, epilogue). He haunts the S & H every night. He cannot eat. He chooses the table near the telephone booth, and makes a scene when he can't get it. He waits. Waits. Waits. Overtips. The manager is thinking of him. These refugees are polite. What fate awaits him? (A gas oven?) The refugees recognize him as a doomed Jew. They shun him. They are the ones who   their way back to life; he cannot. When the restaurant closes, he leaves. He goes to sit on a bench in the island on upper Broadway, where the quiet, broken figures with dogs, the swaying drunks, the feeble and lost souls drift and pass. He is one of them and he cannot ease his torments. He cannot put together the broken fragments of his life. Some time, day or evening, nobody can say when, "the party will call back."

REMEMBRANCE OF CHILDHOOD

I remember a terribly high stoop. Its brown stone steps lead down, down to the dirty gray sidewalk where big kids scramble and shout, playing games. Tough games, too tough for me. Besides, I could never get down there. It is too far away altogether. I sit safely on top of this mountain, chewing a bit of cornbread spread liberally with chicken fat. Delicious. The air smells good. It has rained, and the world is sharp and clear. I wear a sweater and with all the buttons buttoned. And I am smiling, thinking of all the things I am going to do when I am older, maybe tomorrow, and I will be allowed to . . .

*   *   *

My father was a peasant. Transplanted to the stone jungle of Manhattan, he remained a simple, shrewd stubborn peasant. He prospered for a while. Out of sheer industriousness and courage, he carved a niche for himself in the stone, but the tiger of bankruptcy caught up with him and devoured him; he was transformed into human waste by a simple stroke of the economic axe; he became an unwitting symbol of the bankruptcy of a system and a philosophy that has had its day.

*   *   *

My father stood on tippetty-toe. He had to look up to me, and his eyes resented it. "I'm still taller," he said, but he didn't say it to me; he addressed my mother and the grinning mishpurka who were gathered around, pretending to admire my growth, but really deprecating my father. So, he was a runt, eh? He wouldn't give in. He was stubborn. I'm the Boss here, he seemed to say, I'm just like in the Factory. At home, my mother was the Foreman. OK. Boss, she soothed him with a smile.

POP, DID YA BRING HOME ZYMOLE TROKEYS?

(Editors' Note: This outline for a story begins with a poem, followed by notes, and was accompanied by a pencil drawing of a family scene which indicated that Spector may have thought of it for one of his attempts at writing for television. Spector's sister Sara recalls that Zymole Trokeys were throat lozenges of the finest quality, costing 50 cents a package when ordinary cough drops were a nickel. During his prosperous days, their father always had them—possibly because he was a heavy smoker—and always offered them to everyone. They had a bitter sweet taste.)

mood begins gaslit or soon after gaslit; era of hope
long hours of work for the old man, home at night with
fresh sweetsmelling newspapers and the much despised
zymole trokeys, which couldn't hold a chanuka candle to
the jawbreakers and licorice-eyed lollypops I loved

how we were the family; all of us in gayety and harmony together, especially younger kids in marked contrast to mysterious growth-problems of older ones. Benny. introduction of a note of tragedy. mimi nursing at the breast

This short story will revolve about an incident in which B. figures; into which I, kid brother, am drawn without knowledge of its connotations, but with intuitive sense come to full consciousness of import. I the narrator. the incident may be 1) Benny's quitting school by going off by self in dream (A WALK IN THE SNOW)

FRAGMENT OF FAMILY MEMORY (A DREAM)

VERSION A

The blow is struck. Benny reels backward, his lip bleeding at the corner. The blood trickles to his chin and I wonder idly why it is so red. I have always thought that I should fear the sight of blood. Why does it leave me indifferent now? Not fear, but some vague torment moves within me; it has nothing to do with physical violence. I am sorrowful for someone, for everyone in this cursed family. The face of my mother disappears. Benny has tears in his eyes, which blink rapidly. Soon he, too, becomes faint and gray, and vanishes altogether. I confront my father. He is abstracted, reaches into his vest pocket for a cigar, takes a nickel-plated cutter from another pocket, clips the cigar's end, sticks it in his mouth beneath the carefully tended moustache, strikes a safety match, puffs strongly, and throws away the burnt matchstick. He is sitting in his armchair at the head of the dining room table, alone, deserted by the other members of the family (I vaguely remember sisters, shifting silhouettes across a Chinese screen, but how many or what they were like does not interest me; all I sense of them are figures in a crowd which move about in all the rooms of the house, but do not exist as faces or people), and as my father pulls long puffs of satisfaction from his cigar, his long, intelligent nose crinkles with enjoyment and amusement; he is thinking of all the fun he had when he was a kid in Russia, and galloped his horse smartly up grassy slopes, swooping down to pluck a long-stemmed flower, catching himself just in time, and the horse stumbling into a badger's hole and he is thrown, rolls, but recovers rapidly, remounts, and rides on again . . . His head nods, nods, the cigar is crushed in the glass ashtray and his collar is loose, his lip sags, his eyelids close, he is tired. He falls asleep . . .

The snores of my father's pervade the universe of my childhood; like the distant rumbling of mysterious fate it comes through the fuzzy blanket of night in rhythms and accents reminiscent of synagogue prayers. Those distasteful days, my mother dragging me off to *shul*, compelling me to sit and stand by her side as she sits or rises with the rest, and her lips move murmuringly to the nasal tones of the men, the whiners. The men whine and sway back and forth, cry out and wail in a strange singsong fashion, too fast to make sense, too fast to be sincere. . . .

VERSION B

The blow is a heavy one. Benny's head is snapped back, and blood trickles from his lip. The sight of blood makes me sick. Some vague torment writhes within me that has nothing to do with fear. It is pity, pity for every member of this accursed family that is so divided and contemptuous of itself. Now Benny, pale as a ghost, blinks away the tears in his eyes. He does not move, just folds his arms and draws his lips tight. He and my mother become gray, amorphous, and disappear.

I am confronted by my father. Abstracted, he does not see me. He is sitting in the old high-backed chair, the one with arm rests, at the head of the table. He reaches into a vest pocket for a fine long cigar, takes a nickel-plated cutter at the end of his watch chain and clips it neatly. Then he lights up, scratching the match on his pants and tossing the burnt stick onto a plate that serves for an ashtray. He is tired, very tired.

Vaguely, I remember many sisters, shifting silhouettes across a Chinese screen, but what they are like or how many does not interest. My father is thinking of them now, however. They represent the solace and devotion he sorely needs; not rivalry, not threat. His plans for them are grandiose. They need do nothing but obey and be worshipful and he will see that they are fixed for life. They are the daughters of the king, they are Lear's daughters, his diamonds. He draws long puffs of satisfaction from the cigar, and his nose crinkles with enjoyment. Now he thinks of his lighthearted childhood in the Ukraine. He is galloping a splendid horse smartly over the grassy slopes. He swoops to pluck a flower, and the horse stumbles in a gopher hole. He is tumbling, flying over the graceful silken neck, rolling in the dewy sward, up again at once, abreast of the recovered horse, remounted, and away he goes at a gallop again. Tired, tired, he loosens his collar, puts away the cigarbutt and nods, propped up on his elbows, eyelids closed. He is asleep. . . .

My father's snoring fills the universe of my childhood with the distant rumble of mysterious fate.

BENNY'S FUNERAL

The day was misty-black, and raw with wind and rain.
(or)
The day was raw, wet, dark-gray all over.

We had come in a lumping, rickety taxi, following the hearse. Its ancient motor coughed and spluttered; its gears groaned complainingly; its wheels turned corners perilously. We were silent all.

"It's like a dream," my father said. His eyes fluttered like wounded birds.

At the grave, the black velvet coverlet was removed, and the unpainted pine coffin was lifted by gnarled hands and deposited at the grave's edge. Ropes were expertly tied around it and it was lowered, bumping against the dirt sides for an interminable time. Then it rested at the bottom, and the rope came up.

Sleet struck like a knife. The soft slap of earth could be heard falling on the wood of the coffin, as shovelful after shovelful fell. It was as if earth were impatient, greedy for the meal. Somewhere in the air about us there was a great shuddering. This poor corpse, this lost one, had mourners. Fingers of love reached into the soft earth to caress his pale brow. A man had died, had taken fifteen years to die, utterly.

A PERSONAL REVELATION

When my brother died, it was the end of something in me, the end of hope. I dragged my feet through life like a person without identity, without a reason to exist. Faced with evil and threat, as every aspiring human must be in this howling jungle, I ran away. I had to turn back to the childhood that had been so happy before the crashing-to-dust of my revered brother ended it forever. Perhaps, secretly, I believed myself also dead. It troubled me that anything was still expected of me. So I imposed exile and silence upon myself, asking only to be anonymous and forgotten. I was a suicide of the spirit, of whom there must be millions wandering about in the dark corners of this earth.

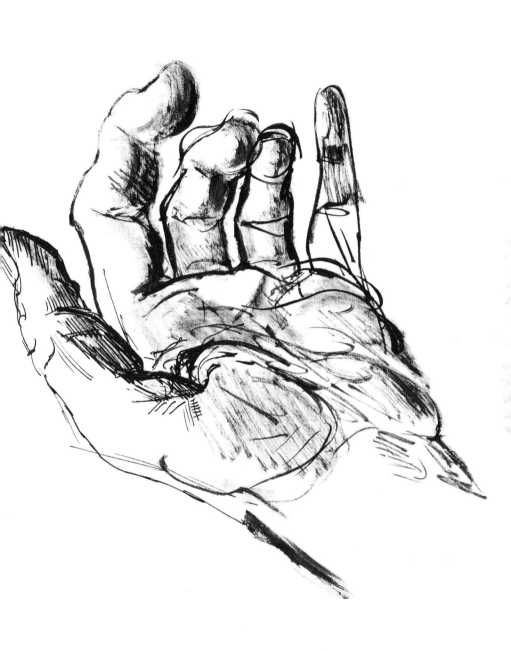

ARTIST INTO STONE

for my brother

Not these dark rooms
Nor smudge of curtains on a screen
Nor gestures of the frenzied hand
Nor trains that grind and roll between
Nor all the throbbing in the brain
Nor tension, cowering from that voice,
Can rise in lightnings to the sky
Can rumble over shuddering earth
Can blast those gents from sloughs of slime
Can pierce them in their swivel chairs
Can slice one second from their busy time . . .
For theirs is the indifference,
Theirs is the kingdom, and the pence.
    Am not my brother's keeper
    Not my brother's corpse
    He in a plain box sleeping
    But I thought I heard him cough;
    The face is pinched and blue,
    The eyes are slits of white,
    The curious stubble of his beard
    Shall flourish through this night . . .
And it is true he died
In throes of vertigo:
He cried, "Is Hitler dead?"
The streets were swathed in snow;
The years were stones, not bread,
Fear stabbed him in the side . . .
    Now fold the weary arm,
    Shutter the staring eye,
    Intone, with syllables of ice,
    The song that does not die.

Though he, the mime, is gone,
The waif who died too soon,
Whose laughter and whose brush recalled
The slum, the stone, the afternoon.
For him, these words of ice;
From him, a flambeau thrown
Far into evening space . . .
Where millioned streets lie stark and still,
All humming underneath.

Acknowledgments

The maiden name of one of this volume's editors is Judith Spector and she first thought of collecting her father's work. The thought was reinforced when, after moving to California, she was introduced to Kenneth Rexroth who asked if she could be related to Herman Spector. Learning that she was Spector's younger daughter he expounded at length on the forgotten writer's influence on Rexroth and others from the period.

George Oppen was helpful and encouraging in many ways, including his insistence of the importance of including fragments of unpublished work which, regardless of their quality in some cases, would show the turmoil in Spector's creative life.

Many others made contributions, by providing memories of the man, helping search for long-forgotten pieces of published work and, in some cases, responding with warmth about the project even though they had no pertinent recollections or missing publications. In only a few instances did they know that Judith was Spector's daughter.

Because it is impossible to credit acknowledgments in proportion to their contribution we are resorting to an alphabetical list but adding special thanks to Spector's sister, Sara Feigenbaum, for her memories and many hours of research assistance; his widow, Clara; his daughter, Sylvia Manson; Joseph Vogel; and Albert Halper, Saul Levitt, and Norman Macleod, for particularly helpful communications, and

Daniel Aaron; Nelson Algren; Harold Anton; Charles L. Babcock, Ohio State University; Cedric Belfrage; Bernard A. Bernier, Jr., and Robert H. Land of the Library of Congress; Alvah Bessie; Mrs. Benjamin Botkin; Kay Boyle; Bob Brown and Phyllis Henrici of the Harris Collection at Brown University's Library; Stanley Burnshaw; Patricia K. Clatanoff of the University of Chicago's Joseph Regenstein Library; Sue Considine; Jack Conroy; Alan Covici, University of California Library; Pawel J. Depta, Harvard College Library; Pele de Lappe; Bascha De Ward; Robert W. Dunn; Ralph Ellison; Morris Ernst; Mr. and Mrs. Lou Farber; James T. Farrell; Ben

Field; Michael Folsom; Barron M. Franz, New York Public Library; R. W. Fromm, New York State Historical Association;

Donald Gallup and Kenneth Neisheim, Yale University's Beinecke Rare Book and Manuscript Library; Sender Garlin; Karl Gay, Lockwood Library Poetry Room at State University of New York at Buffalo; Larry Gellert; John Gildersleeve; Henry Gilfond; W. Goldwater; Louis Grudin; Allen Guttman; Curtis Harnack, Yaddo; Diana Haskell, The Newberry Library; Alfred Hayes; Hoover Institution at Stanford University; Irving Howe; Mrs. Richard Humeston (widow of Mike Gold); Leo Hurwitz; Carolyn Jakeman, Harvard University's Houghton Library; Theo Jung; Aaron Kramer; Cordell Klyne, University of Wisconsin Memorial Library; Mrs. Alfred Kreymborg; James Laughlin; Sally Leach, University of Texas Library; Shelley Lemon, San Francisco Public Library; Denise Levertov; Kenneth A. Lohf and Eugene P. Sheehy, Columbia University Libraries; Philip Lyman; Eugene Lyons;

Dwight Macdonald; David Madden; Ben Maddow; A. B. Magil; Albert Maltz; Jerre Mangione; Irwin Mayers, Merritt College Library; R. Russell Maylone, Northwestern University Library; Tom McGrath; Lewis Mumford; Steve Murdock; Sally M. Neely, University of Cincinnati Library; Edward Newhouse; Linda Oppenheim, Princeton University Library; Mrs. Kenneth Patchen;

Carl Rakosi; Harry Raskőlenko; Naomi Replansky; Al Richmond; Mary Rolfe; Jerome Rothenberg, University of Wisconsin-Milwaukee; Annette Rubinstein; Muriel Rukeyser; Marion Sader; Jack Salzman, Long Island University; Arthur Scharf; Isidor Schneider; Edgar Shapiro; Eileen Sheahan, Yale University Library; Miriam and Wilfrid Sheed; Bernard Smith; Walter Snow; Marjorie C. Toomer; Parker Tyler; Ted Wilentz; Louis Zukofsky.

It was stated earlier that there was no known publication of Spector between the excerpt in *Scientific American* in 1963 and this volume, but this is not totally accurate. Five Spector poems were published by his granddaughter Jane Manson in a hand-printed edition of 25 at Mills College's Eucalyptus Press in 1976. Also, some of his work is included in recent reprint editions of little magazines for which he wrote.

The drawings of Herman Spector reproduced in this book are from the collections of his daughters Judith and Sylvia, and his sister Sara. The mediums used were pen and ink, pencil and charcoal.